INTR

The Peninsular War fou   uese
and Spanish on one side, and tl   ı the
other, is one of the most fascinating conflicts ...   / the
British army. Against the odds, Wellington's small force of redcoats
achieved victory after victory. They took on and defeated the most
feared army of their time, and Wellington continually bested
Napoleon's elite marshals.

This is the second volume of my history of the war. In volume
one, I wrote how the much-maligned British army won its spurs at the
battles of Roliça, Vimeiro, Porto and Talavera. In this volume, we see
that army come of age and develop its tremendous confidence at
battles such as Bussaco, Barossa and the bloodiest battle of the war –
Albuera.

My goal in writing this series is to draw attention to the
redcoats who made up one of the greatest and most effective armies
that Britain has ever fielded – men like William Grattan of the 88th
Regiment of Foot (The Connaught Rangers), Robert Blakeney of the
28th Regiment of Foot and August Schaumann of the King's German
Legion. I have quoted extensively from the large number of wonderful
memoirs that men like these have left for us. As well as the French,
these soldiers battled a lack of food, extreme cold, tremendous heat,
and sickness that claimed the lives of thousands. I am a strong
believer that history comes alive through the accounts of those who
were there, and so this book, like my others, is very much a 'bottom-
up' account of the Peninsular War. It is a work that focuses on the
experiences of the lower-ranks and junior officers – the men who
endured the fighting. They deserve to be remembered, and their
stories brought to a new generation of military history enthusiasts.

The structure of the book is a simple narrative history, but if
you want more information on the subjects covered, then please be
sure to read the appendices for supplemental material. Appendix One
gives the British order of battle for each of the major engagements
covered in the book, while Appendix Two gives further information

on the recruitment, organisation, and tactics of the British infantry. I have also included the transcripts of many interviews with experts, including the wonderful Dr Mark Thompson, Marcus de la Poer Beresford (a distant relative of Marshal William Carr Beresford) and Marcus Cribb the former manager of Wellington's Apsley House in London. I owe these brilliant historians an enormous debt of gratitude.

It is my mission in life to preserve and promote the study of the British military history, therefore please be sure to subscribe to my Redcoat History Podcast and YouTube channel where I post regular interviews on all aspects of British military history. I also highly recommend that you sign up for my mailing list to receive your monthly despatch that includes links to a plethora of interesting articles and videos that you will enjoy. Links for all of these can be found via the QR code below – just scan it with your phone camera.

A special thanks, as always, is due to my tireless editor Chris Biggs. Chris is a busy man with a family and a fulltime job, but he is always willing to help and advise me. Any mistakes that remain in this book are purely my own stubborn fault.

A CHRONOLOGY OF THE EVENTS COVERED IN THIS BOOK

20 October 1809: *Construction begins on the Lines of Torres Vedras.*

5 February 1810: *The French Siege of Cadiz begins.*

19 March 1810: *The skirmish at Barba del Puerco. The men of the 95th Rifles repulse an attack by General Claude Françoise Ferey.*

26 April 1810: The *French begin the first siege of Ciudad Rodrigo.*

10 July 1810: *Ciudad Rodrigo finally falls to the French after a lengthy and stubborn resistance by the Spanish garrison.*

24 July 1810: *The Battle of the Coa River. In this action, General Robert Craufurd and his Light Brigade are caught on the eastern side*

of the Coa River, outside of Almeida, and forced into a fighting retreat.

25 July 1810: *The First Siege of Almeida begins.* French *Marshal Michel Ney surrounds the Allied garrison.*

27 August 1810: *Almeida surrenders to the French after an enormous explosion in the magazine causes chaos and massive casualties amongst the defenders.*

27 September 1810: *The Battle of Bussaco is fought. The British and Portuguese armies, under Wellington, successfully repulse multiple attacks by the French under Marshal Masséna. The next day the Allied flank is turned, and Wellington orders his men to withdraw.*

14 October 1810: *The Battle of Sobral. At this battle, a French force unsuccessfully probes the Lines of Torres Vedras.*

26 January 1811: *The French, under the command of Marshal Soult, start besieging the border-city of Badajoz.*

19 February 1811: *The Battle of Gebora, outside of Badajoz, sees a Spanish army crushed.*

3 March 1811: *Marshal Masséna begins his retreat from Santarem.*

5 March 1811: *The Battle of Barrosa is fought outside of Cadiz. Sergeant Masterson captures a French Imperial Eagle.*

25-26 March 1811: *The Battle of Campo Mayor (also known as Campo Maior).*

3 April 1811: *The Battle of Sabugal. The Allied army attack the isolated French 2nd Corps as they retreat from Portugal.*

11 April 1811: *Marshal Masséna and his emaciated army reach*

6

Salamanca, marking the end of their retreat.

12 April 1811*: British blockade of Almeida begins.*

3-5 May 1811: *The Battle of Fuentes de Oñoro. In this punishing battle, Wellington and his army block Marshal Masséna's attempt to breakthrough to Almeida. The French retreat on the 6th of May.*

6 May 1811*: An Allied army under the command of Marshal William Carr Beresford begins the First Allied Siege of Badajoz.*

11 May 1811*: Marshal Marmont replaces Marshal Masséna as the commander of the Army of Portugal.*

12 May 1811: *Marshal Beresford lifts the Siege of Badajoz to confront Marshal Soult's army, which is advancing to its relief.*

16 May 1811: *The Battle of Albuera. In this horrific battle, Marshal Beresford's Allied army blocks Marshal Soult from relieving Badajoz. As a percentage of those involved, this was the bloodiest battle of the Peninsular War.*

25 May 1811: *Major General Houston's 7th Division begins the investment of Badajoz, marking the beginning of the second British siege of the city.*

10 June 1811: *After two failed assaults, Wellington abandons the Siege of Badajoz.*

25 September 1811: *The Battle of El Bodon. The Allied army fights a rear-guard action against a much larger French force under Marshal Marmont.*

28 October 1811: *The Battle of Arroyo dos Molinos. General Rowland Hill's 2nd Division surprises and routs an entire French division*

under the command of General Jean Baptiste Girard.

CHAPTER ONE: THE THIRD FRENCH INVASION OF PORTUGAL

THE COMBAT AT THE COA RIVER – 24TH OF JULY 1810

It was just after dawn on the 24th of July 1810 when the French advanced. First came the cavalry, emerging from the gloom to chase away the British pickets who were drenched from the night's storm. Then came an immense column of over 20,000 infantrymen – drums beating and Imperial Eagles raised proudly above them. Facing the French were 5,000 men of the elite Light Division, commanded by Brigadier General Robert *'Black Bob'* Craufurd. He had been warned by his Commander-in-Chief, Lieutenant General Wellesley – now known as Wellington of Talavera and Baron Douro, not to dally on the east bank of the Coa River and to avoid a major engagement. Craufurd had ignored his commanding officer's instructions and had instead maintained his division's position outside the walls of the Portuguese fortress-city of Almeida. To exacerbate his weakness, the ground was not favourable to him – there was a steep defile, and a swollen river in his rear.

Marshal Michel Ney, a brave and experienced soldier, commanded the advancing French 6th Corps. Ney immediately recognised that Craufurd's men were in an exposed and dangerous situation. If the French could manoeuvre quickly, they could annihilate the Allied troops, force a crossing over the River Coa and cut-off Almeida.

As the dense, blue-coated columns marched relentlessly forward, the riflemen of the 95th Rifles, along with the men of the 43rd and 52nd Regiments of Foot and the Portuguese Caçadores, quickly engaged them with their rifles and muskets. General Craufurd, caught ill-prepared, struggled to maintain command and control of his division. The French gradually forced the Allied troops back across the broken ground, struggling to keep order amongst the rocks, walls, and vineyards. A young subaltern of the 95th, George Simmons, later recalled:

> The whole plain in our front was covered with horse and foot advancing towards us. The enemy's infantry formed line and, with an innumerable multitude of skirmishers, attacked us fiercely; we repulsed them; they came on again, yelling, with drums beating, frequently the drummers leading, often in front of the line, French officers like mountebanks running forward and placing their hats upon their swords, and capering about like madmen, saying, as they turned to their men, 'Come on, children of our country. The first that advances, Napoleon will recompense him.' Numbers returned to the attack. We kept up a very brisk fire. Several guns began to play upon us, and as the force kept increasing every moment in our front, and columns of infantry were also moving upon our right flank, we were ordered to retire half the company. Captain O'Hare's retired, and the remainder, under Lieutenant Johnston, still remained fighting for a few moments longer. I was with this party. We moved from the field into the road, our men falling all round us, when a body of Hussars in bearskin caps and light-coloured pelisses got amongst the few remaining Riflemen and began to sabre them. Several attempted to cut me down, but I avoided their kind intentions by stepping on one side. I had a large cloak rolled up and strapped across my body; my haversack was filled with little necessary articles for immediate use; thus, I got clear off. A volley was now fired by a party of the 43rd under Captain Wells, which brought several of the Hussars to the ground. In the scuffle I took to my heels and ran to the 43rd, Wells calling out, 'Mind the Rifle Man! Do not hit him, for heaven's sake.' As I was compelled to run into their fire to escape, he seized me by the hand and was delighted beyond measure at my escape. The road to a small bridge across the Coa, which the Division would have to retire over, was very bad and rocky. Our gallant fellows disputed manfully every inch of ground and retired towards the river. [1]

It was then that Simmons was wounded – a musket ball smashing into his thigh and knocking him over. A nearby Sergeant probably saved his life by applying a tourniquet made from a handkerchief and a ramrod.

The eminent historian of the Peninsular War, William Napier, was a captain with the 52nd Regiment of Foot during the fight. He picks up the story:

> As the retiring troops approached the river, they came upon a more open space; but the left wing being harder pressed, and having the shortest distance, arrived while the bridge was still crowded and some of the right wing distant. Major M'Leod, of the 43rd, seeing this, rallied four companies on a hill just in front of the passage, and was immediately joined by a party of the 95th; and at the same time two other companies were posted by Brigade-Major Rowan, on another hill flanking the road. These posts were maintained until the enemy, gathering in great numbers, made a second burst, when the companies fell back; but at that moment the right wing of the 52nd was seen marching towards the bridge, which was still crowded with the passing troops. M'Leod, a very young man, but with a natural genius for war, immediately turned his horse around, called to the troops to follow, and, taking off his cap, rode with a shout towards the enemy. The suddenness of the thing, and the distinguished action of the man, produced the effect he desired; a mob of soldiers rushed after him, cheering and charging as if the whole army had been at their backs, and the enemy skirmishers, astonished at this unexpected movement, stopped short. Before they could recover from their surprise, the 52nd crossed the river, and M'Leod, following at full speed, also gained the other side without disaster.[2]

Captain Jonathan Leach of the 95th, a veteran of Roliça and Vimeiro, recalled:

> The whole of General Craufurd's corps at length gained the opposite bank of the Coa, and was strongly posted near the bridge, behind walls, rocks and broken ground. The torrents of rain which fell the night before had so swollen the river, that all the fords were at that moment impassable; a fortunate circumstance, as the only way by which we could now be attacked was over the narrow bridge, on which we could bring a destructive fire.[3]

In a private letter to a friend, Lieutenant Henry Booth of the 43rd continued:

> We defended the bridge against three attempts of the French to

force it, in all of which they failed, suffering heavy loss. At last the firing mutually ceased, on account of the torrents of rain that fell, after five hours hard peppering at each other. Towards night we retired, and have been gradually falling back. . .The main body of the army is still more in the rear and we have only a few cavalry in our front.[4]

It had been a hard morning's fighting for the men of the Light Division, who had nearly paid a terrible price for Craufurd's unwillingness to withdraw them rapidly across the Coa River. Wellington's displeasure at the affair is clear from a letter he wrote to his brother immediately afterwards:

You may be very certain that not only have I had nothing to do with, but had positively forbidden, the foolish affair in which Craufurd involved his outposts. . .I had positively desired him not to engage in any affair on the other side of the Coa; and as soon as La Concepcion was blown up on the 21st, I had expressed my wish that he should withdraw his infantry to the left of the river; and I repeated my injunction that he should not engage in an affair on the right of the river.[5]

Craufurd, a man of immense talents and much respected by Wellington, had been too eager to risk his division in an unnecessary fight. It seems likely that he was desperate to prove himself after a career that had been full of misfortune and missed opportunities. That night, under the cover of darkness, the division finally withdrew, falling back towards the town of Pinhel. The third French Invasion of Portugal was now in full swing.

BACKGROUND TO THE THIRD FRENCH INVASION

It had been nearly a year since the last major battle fought by the British Expeditionary Force in the Peninsular. The Battle of Talavera in July 1809 had been a brutal one, and the subsequent retreat from Spain in the autumn had been arduous.[6] The British army, already much weakened, was then ravaged by disease. An illness known by the troops as Guadiana Fever had swept through them, killing over 500 men a month throughout the winter.[7] Sergeant John Spencer Cooper of the 2nd Battalion 7th Royal Fusiliers, a veteran of Talavera, was one of the sick. His symptoms included a loss of hearing and of appetite, terrible blisters on his back and feet and a fever that sometimes left him *'insensible.'* Along with many others, he was transported to a hospital in the Portuguese fortress city of Elvas. Here, the squalid conditions and poor standard of medical care did not bode well for a speedy recovery. Sergeant Cooper later recalled:

> Into bomb-proof barracks again. No ventilation, twenty sick men in the room, of whom about eighteen died. In this place there were one door and one chimney, but no windows. Relapse again; deaf as a post; shirt unchanged and sticking to my sore back; ears running stinking matter; a man lying close on my right hand, with both his legs mortified nearly to the knees, and dying. A little sympathy would have soothed, but sympathy there was none. The orderlies (men who acted as nurses to the sick) were brutes.[8]

While the men tried to recover their health, Wellington set about organising the defence of Portugal against the inevitable return of the French. Whether Portugal could be defended or not had been a long-standing debate amongst the British commanders and politicians. General Sir John Moore, who had commanded the Expeditionary Force during their advance into Spain, which had ended in the terrible retreat to Corunna in January 1809, judged that Portugal could not be defended. Wellington disagreed and believed that there were three key elements to defending the country.

The first was to turn the Portuguese army into a strong, legitimate force that could be trusted to hold its own against the French columns. For this job, Lord William Carr Beresford, an experienced British commander who spoke fluent Portuguese, was given command of the Portuguese army, with the local rank of marshal. He could see that the Portuguese forces had potential – the new recruits were patriotic, brave, and keen for a crack at the French; but many of the older, senior officers lacked the skills and knowledge necessary to lead them. Beresford therefore embedded British officers within the Portuguese regiments to improve their training and teach the less-experienced Portuguese officers the skills required to command. British drill was also implemented, and they formed rifle regiments called *Caçadores* along British lines. By the end of 1809, Beresford's efforts were already paying dividends as Lieutenant August Schaumann, a Deputy Assistant Commissary-General with the cavalry of the King's German Legion recalled:

> The Portuguese army had been so thoroughly put in order. . .that it was possible to incorporate her strong, well-drilled, finely equipped regiments in the English army. These fellows, with their dark brown faces, really looked quite martial.[9]

The second element of Wellington's plan was to build a line of fortifications that would protect Lisbon and stop a French advance in its tracks. This would come to be known as the Lines of Torres Vedras, and we will discover more about this incredible engineering feat in chapter three.

The third element of Wellington's plan to defend Portugal hinged on a scorched earth policy that would leave nothing useful for the invaders. Food was to be destroyed, and all cattle slaughtered or driven off. Roads and bridges were to be demolished. Portuguese civilians would be forced to move behind the Lines of Torres Vedras or take to the hills and hide. This scorched earth policy, as brutal as it was for the local population, was crucial to Wellington's plan.

MARSHAL MASSÉNA TAKES COMMAND

While the British were building forts and training the Portuguese, the French were busy preparing and reorganising their army in the Peninsular. After Napoleon Bonaparte's decisive victory over the Austrians at Wagram in July 1809, he began sending more troops to Spain. Many of these soldiers were veterans – full of confidence after their recent victories in central Europe.

For a while it was assumed that the Emperor would come to Spain and take command of the army, but personal and political events in Paris meant he decided against it. It is also likely that

Napoleon could see that the war in the Peninsular would never bring him an easy victory – playing *whack-a-mole* with the brutal Guerillas who harried his lines of communication was not his idea of glory. Instead, he sent one of the most experienced and cunning of all his Marshals', Andre Masséna, the Prince of Essling.

Marshal Masséna was an army veteran who had come up through the ranks during the early stages of the revolution. There was no doubt about his military talents. He had an impressive track record, but he was also renowned for his love of plunder. At 52 years old, he was showing his age. He had grown thin, stooped and was blind in his left eye – shot by Napoleon during a hunting accident. His recent campaigns had left him physically and mentally exhausted.

When Masséna arrived in Spain to take up his command, he told his officers: 'Gentlemen, I am here contrary to my own wish; I begin to feel myself too old and too weary to go on active service. The Emperor says that I must, and replied to the reasons for declining this post which I gave him, by saying that my reputation would suffice to end the war. It was very flattering no doubt, but no man has two lives to live on this earth—the soldier least of all.'[10]

To make Masséna's new assignment harder, Napoleon stopped short of giving him full command of the various corps currently active across Spain. He was only to command the so-called Army of Portugal – which comprised three corps of around 138,000 men in total. This meant that should his force need help, Masséna couldn't simply order the other Marshals to his aid. This lack of a local Commander-in-Chief was incredibly problematic for French strategy, but it allowed Napoleon to micro-manage his marshals from Paris and force them to rely on him. Napoleon had also placed his brother Joseph on the Spanish throne, but had given him little actual power. This bizarre and counter-productive French system in the Peninsular was already tearing at the seams. As Wellington wrote to his brother: 'This is not the way in which they have conquered Europe. There is something discordant in all the French arrangements for Spain. Joseph divides his Kingdom into *préfetures*, while Napoleon parcels it out into governments; Joseph makes a great military expedition into

15

the south of Spain and undertakes the siege of Cadiz, while Napoleon places all the troops and half the kingdom under the command of Massena and calls it the Army of Portugal.'[11]

BARBA DEL PUERCO, 19th OF MARCH 1810

As winter passed into spring, the two sides began probing each other's strength and weaknesses along the Portuguese border. On the night of 19th of March 1810, General Claude Françoise Ferey led his troops in a surprise attack against the small British outpost at Barba del Puerco on the River Agueda.

Thick dark clouds blocked the moonlight, and heavy rain concealed the noise of the French advance. A stone bridge, built by the Romans – four meters wide and 90 meters long – spanned the river with a narrow zig-zag track running from both ends up the steep hillsides. The French skirmishers advanced carefully, using their bayonets to kill the unfortunate green-jacketed sentry. The leading Frenchmen stepped over his body and advanced at the double before being spotted by another sharp-eyed British rifleman of the 95th Rifles, his powder dry despite the downpour. The greenjacket raised the rifle butt to his shoulder and pulled the trigger. It was a rushed shot, but the noise and muzzle flash had done their duty and the small British outpost at Barba Del Puerco was now awake and alert to the danger.

As the clouds briefly parted, the moonlight revealed 600 Frenchmen swarming across the bridge, with a further 1,500 in reserve behind. George Simmons recalled:

> A small party [of riflemen] stationed amongst the rocks kept up a fire. The sergeant being shot through the mouth and the enemy being so numerous, they could not impede their progress. In a moment, after the arrival of the main body of the piquet, the French were literally scrambling up the rocky ground within ten yards of us. We commenced firing at each other very spiritedly. Their drums beat a charge, and the French attempted to dislodge us without effect. My friend, Lieutenant Mercer, who was putting on his spectacles, received a musket ball through his head, and

fell dead close to my feet. Several were now falling, and the moon for a few minutes shone brightly, then disappeared, and again at intervals let us see each other. We profited by this circumstance, as their belts were white and over their greatcoats, so that where they crossed upon the breast, combined with the glare of the breast-plate, gave a grand mark for our rifles. Our men being in dark dresses, and, from their small number, obliged to keep close together, the ground also being exceedingly rugged, were all favourable circumstances. We fought in this way for at least half an hour against fearful odds, when Lieutenant Colonel Beckwith brought up the three reserve companies from the village, who soon decided the affair. The enemy was driven in the greatest confusion back over frightful precipices, leaving two officers killed and a number of men wounded.[12]

As outpost battles like this continued along the border, Wellington tried to understand which of the available routes the French would use to invade so that he could deploy his army accordingly. But Masséna dawdled, taking his time before eventually moving against the walled Spanish border-city of Ciudad Rodrigo. The city covers the northern invasion route into Portugal and was defended by 5,000 Spanish troops. The Spaniards put up a brave resistance for ten weeks before finally surrendering. This stubborn fight by the Spanish brought Wellington valuable time, allowing him to make his own defensive dispositions. In late July the French finally advanced in large numbers, determined to sweep aside the Allies and conquer Portugal once and for all.

THE SIEGE OF ALMEIDA, JULY/AUGUST 1810

After the combat on the Coa and the withdrawal of Craufurd's Light Division, related at the start of the chapter, Masséna settled down to besiege the nearby fortress city of Almeida. Sieges were incredibly difficult undertakings for an army. They would soak up huge numbers of troops and artillery. Entire campaigns would often hinge on a swift and successful outcome.

Almeida promised to be a tough nut to crack. The fortress was a solidly built star-shaped structure defended by nearly 5,000

17

Portuguese troops – mainly militia men. The garrison was commanded by British Brigadier General William Cox. Wellington hoped Almeida would hold out for at least two months, delaying the French until the heavy autumn rains, which would make any further French advance much more difficult.

By the 24th of August, the French finally had 50 guns in position.[13] As the siege begun, excellent counter-battery fire from the defenders hampered their bombardment. The French also discovered that digging trenches was slow, back-breaking work because of the hard, rocky ground that surrounded the city.

The situation looked promising for the Allies until a freak accident changed everything. During the evening of the 26th of August, a French bomb fell in the castle's courtyard, which was being used as the central powder magazine. Thanks to terrible bad luck, the bomb ignited a powder trail that ran through the open door into the magazine. The subsequent explosion was catastrophic for the defenders. A French witness to the explosion recalled:

> The earth trembled, and we saw an immense whirlwind of fire and smoke rise from the middle of the place. It was like the bursting of a volcano—one of the things that I can never forget after twenty-six years. Enormous blocks of stone were hurled into the trenches, where they killed and wounded some of our men. Guns of heavy calibre were lifted from the ramparts and hurled down far outside them. When the smoke cleared off, a great part of Almeida had disappeared, and the rest was a heap of débris.[14]

Five hundred of the defenders were killed instantly, including nearly all the artillerymen. Despite this disaster, General Cox was determined to carry on the defence of the city for as long as possible, but his garrison was now demoralised and demanded that he surrender. He had little choice but to comply, and on the morning of the 28th of August 1810, the garrison marched out of the city into captivity. The road into the interior of Portugal was now open for Masséna and his army, which now numbered around 65,000 soldiers.

CHAPTER TWO: THE BATTLE OF BUSSACO

The premature fall of Almeida meant Wellington had to act quickly. The civilian population was now ordered to retreat with all their belongings towards Lisbon, while Wellington had his engineers destroy all the roads that the French might use.

Before he withdrew his army into their newly built defensive *Lines of Torres Vedras* north of Lisbon, Wellington hoped to give Masséna's army a bloody nose which would boost his men's morale and prove to the pessimistic politicians in London that his army was still capable of victory. He found the perfect place to make his stand on a long ridge at a place called Bussaco.

The ridge, eight miles north-east of the town of Coimbra, is an imposing feature that rises 200m from the valley floor. Nowhere can it be easily climbed – the steep slopes covered with heather and rocks.

By the morning of the 26th of September, the British and Portuguese armies were concentrated and in position on the reverse slope of the ten-mile long ridge. Wellington had just over 50,000 troops – around half of them British, the rest mainly Portuguese. This would be a splendid chance for the Portuguese to win their spurs and prove how much they had improved as a fighting force since the dark days of 1807 and 1808.

William Tomkinson, a young cavalry officer with the 16th Light Dragoons, summed up the British feelings when he wrote in his diary on September 26th:

> At 2 p.m.. . .the whole army was in position along the Sierra. . .The enemy have closed up their whole force to the hills in front of the position, and a general action is expected. From the nature of our position, I cannot think the enemy will make any serious attack. The descent in places is so steep and great that a person alone cannot, without holding and choosing his ground, get down. I cannot think they will be so imprudent as to make it a general affair. . .The army is in most beautiful order, and the Portuguese as fine-looking men and as steady under arms as any in the world. The only doubt rests with them; if they do their duty, and the business becomes general, there can be no doubt of

success.[15]

Wellington had to husband his troops to defend the key points. He positioned the bulk of his regiments along the three roads along which he expected the French to advance. He had an advantage because from the top of the ridge he could see the French dispositions while keeping his own men well hidden behind the crest. This meant that Marshal Masséna could not be certain of the size or position of the Anglo-Portuguese force. Wellington instructed his commanders that the men were to be kept out of sight until needed to repel an attack. This was a classic Wellington tactic that he would deploy frequently throughout his career.

Wellington's right wing was anchored on the Mondego River, and here he positioned Major General Rowland 'Daddy' Hill's 2nd Division. To Hill's left was the 5th Division of Major General James Leith, which included two Portuguese Brigades. There was then a long gap in the line between Leith's division and the 3rd Division under Major General Thomas Picton, a brave but divisive figure.[16] The heaviest concentration of men was towards the north end of the ridge around the Bussaco convent and the village of Sula. There Wellington had positioned Major General Brent Spencer's 1st Division and the Light Division. On the extreme left flank, covering the steep slopes, was Major General Lowry Cole's 4th Division, as well as an independent Portuguese Brigade and the King's German Legion. 60 well-placed artillery pieces supported the entire line.

Wellington, professional and highly organised as always, even had a road built that ran laterally along the entire ridge. This would allow him to deploy his forces to and from any point where they might be needed.

The British Commander was confident that his men would hold. But Massena, accustomed to victory, was equally certain that his troops would successfully storm the position. The French Marshal declared, 'I cannot persuade myself that Lord Wellington will risk the loss of a reputation by giving battle, but if he does, I have him! Tomorrow we shall affect the conquest of Portugal, and in a few days, I shall drown the leopard.'[17] Given the terrain, his confidence seems bizarrely misplaced.

THE BATTLE OF BUSSACO
27 SEPTEMBER 1810

On the afternoon of the 26th, Captain Moyle Sherer of the 2/34th Regiment of Foot arrived on the ridge. Filled with curiosity, he went to look at his enemy:

> My regiment had no sooner piled arms than I walked to the verge of the mountain on which we lay, in the hope that I might discover something of the enemy. Little, however, was I prepared for the magnificent scene which burst on my astonished sight. Far

as the eye could stretch, the glittering of steel, and clouds of dust raised by cavalry and artillery, proclaimed the march of a countless army; while immediately below me, at the foot of those precipitous heights on which I stood, their picquets were already posted; thousands of them were already halted in their bivouacs, and column too after column arriving in quick succession, reposed upon the ground allotted to them, and swelled the black and enormous masses. . .This then, was the French army: here lay, before me, the men who had once, for nearly two years, kept the whole coast of England in alarm; who had conquered Italy, overrun Austria, shouted victory on the plains of Austerlitz. . .tomorrow, I may, for the first time hear the din of battle, behold the work of slaughter, share the honours of a hard-fought field, or be numbered with the slain.[18]

That night, the British and Portuguese, forbidden from lighting campfires, did their best to try and sleep under the stars. In some units the morale was low, as August Schaumann remembered:

Our courage, moreover, was not at its best, for an army in retreat is conscious of its weakness and loses confidence in itself and its leaders. Indeed, several English officers were so convinced that we would have to take to our ships that they had already informed their families in England that this was our certain and ineluctable fate.[19]

For many of the men, like Moyle Sherer, this would be their first major battle. Ensign William Grattan of the 88th Connaught Rangers recalled:

At night we lay down to rest; each man, with his firelock in his grasp, remained at his post, anxiously waiting the arrival of the morrow, which was destined to be the last that many amongst us were to behold. We had no fires and the death-like stillness that reigned throughout our army was only interrupted by the occasional challenge of an advanced sentry, or a random shot fired at some imaginary foe. The night at length passed over, but long before the dawn of day the warlike preparations of the enemy were to be heard. The trumpets sounded for the horsemen to prepare for the fight, and the roll of the drums and shrill notes of the fife gave notice to the French infantry that the hour had arrived when its claim to be the best in Europe was to be disputed. On our side all was still as the grave. Lord Wellington lay amongst his soldiers, under no other covering than his cloak, and as he passed through the ranks of the different battalions already formed, his presence and manner gave that confidence to his companions which had a magical effect. All was now ready on our part; the men stood to their arms; and as each soldier took his place in the line, his quiet demeanour, and orderly, but determined appearance, was a strong contrast to the bustle and noise which prevailed amongst our opposite neighbours; but those preparations were of short continuance, and some straggling shots along the brow of the mountain gave warning that we were about to commence the battle of Bussaco.[20]

As the early morning mist cleared on the 27th, Marshal Masséna, hungry for a swift victory, formed his men up and threw them in column formation up the steep slopes towards the waiting redcoats. He had clearly not learned from the French defeats at the battles of Vimeiro, Corunna, and Talavera. The huge, dense columns that had intimidated and smashed their way through armies across Europe did not have the same effect against the steady two-deep line of British redcoats and their rapid volley fire.

THE SOUTHERN SECTOR

First to attack was General Jean Reynier's 2nd Corps – a bulldozer moving west along the central road against Picton's Division. There were eleven French battalions in three regimental formations[21] – an intimidating sight. William Grattan standing nervously in line waiting for the enemy recalled:

The fog cleared away, and a bright sun enabled us to see what was passing before us. A vast crowd of tirailleurs [light troops] were pressing onward with great ardour, and their fire, as well as their numbers, was so superior to that of our advance, that some men of the brigade of Lightburne, as also a few of the 88th Regiment, were killed while standing in line; a colour sergeant named Macnamara was shot through the head close beside myself and Ensign Owgan.[22]

General Éttiene Heudelet de Bierre's column was soon engaged. The heavy musketry of 1/74th Regiment of Foot and the 21st Regiment of the Portuguese army, as well as two batteries of Portuguese artillery, ploughed deep lanes through the blue-coated ranks until they brought it to a bloody standstill. As this was happening, another French column slightly to Heudelet's right - comprising General Pierre Merle's Division was able to exploit a gap in the British line. Showing immense determination and fitness, the French infantry reached the crest of the ridge. Grattan explains what happened next:

> Lord Wellington was no longer to be seen, and Wallace and his regiment, standing alone without orders, had to act for themselves. The Colonel sent his captain of Grenadiers (Dunne) to the right, where the rocks were highest, to ascertain how matters stood, for he did not wish, at his own peril, to quit the ground he had been ordered to occupy without some strong reason for so doing. All this time the brigade of Lightburne, as also the 88th, were standing at ordered arms. In a few moments Dunne returned almost breathless he said the rocks were filling fast with Frenchmen, that a heavy column was coming up the hill beyond the rocks, and that the four companies of the 45th were about to be attacked. Wallace asked if he thought half the 88th would be able to do the business. 'You will want every man,' was the reply. Wallace, with a steady but cheerful countenance, turned to his men, and looking them full in the face, said, 'Now, Connaught Rangers, mind what you are going to do; pay attention to what I have so often told you, and when I bring you face to face with those French rascals, drive them down the hill— don't give the false touch, but push home to the muzzle! I have nothing more to say, and if I had it would be of no use, for in a minute or two there'll be such an infernal noise about your ears that you won't be able to hear yourselves.' This address went home to the hearts of us all, but there was no cheering; a steady but determined calm had taken the place of any lighter feeling, and it seemed as if the men had made up their minds to go to their work unruffled and not too much excited.[23]

And so, Lieutenant Colonel John Wallace with his 88th, alongside the 45th Regiment (the Nottinghams) counter-attacked to push the French off the ridge. They advanced diagonally across the plateau. Grattan continues:

> Wallace threw himself from his horse, and placing himself at the head of the 45th and 88th, with Gwynne of the 45th on the one side of him, and Captain Seton of the 88th on the other, ran forward at a charging pace into the midst of the terrible flame in his front. All was now confusion and uproar, smoke, fire and bullets, officers and soldiers, French drummers and French drums knocked down in every direction; British, French, and Portuguese mixed together while in the midst of all was to be seen Wallace, fighting like his ancestor of old—at the head of his devoted followers, and calling out to his soldiers to 'press forward.' Never was defeat more complete, and it was a proud moment for Wallace and Gwynne when they saw their gallant comrades breaking down and trampling under their feet this splendid division composed of some of the best troops the world could boast of. The leading (French) regiment, the 36th, one of Napoleon's favourite battalions, was nearly destroyed. . .and the face of the hill was strewed with dead and wounded.[24]

The quick thinking and bravery of Colonel Wallace and the redcoats of the Connaught Rangers and the Nottinghams had now broken the French attack in this sector. But the battle was far from over.

Just to the right of Grattan's position, seven French Battalions under General Maximilien Foy were thrown forward. The rest of Picton's Division was too weak and strung out to hold them. But now the communications road that Wellington had had built proved its importance, allowing Leith's 5th Division to march rapidly north along the position to support Picton. In fact, they arrived just as the French crested the ridge. It was perfect timing and immediately the red-coated battalions began pouring fire into the French.

Andrew Leith-Hay, an Ensign of the 29th Regiment of Foot, was nearby and recalled:

> Colonel Barnes' brigade of General Leith's corps, composed of the 3rd Royal Scots [3/1st], 9th, and 38th regiments, had been advanced to the head of the column, and consequently first came in contact

with the enemy; the 9th Regiment, commanded by Colonel Cameron, being the leading battalion, when about a hundred yards distant, wheeled into line, firing a volley, the effect of which was terrific; the ground was covered with dead and dying, not new levies or mercenaries, but the elite of the French army. This destructive fire being followed up by an immediate charge, the enemy gave way, rushing down the steep face of the sierra in the utmost confusion.[25]

General Foy, who was wounded in this engagement, later wrote: 'The head of my column fell back on its right, despite my efforts; I could not get them to deploy. Disorder set in, and the 17th and 70th raced downhill in headlong flight.'[26]

This second French reversal marked the end of the major actions on the southern part of the ridge. Reynier's 2nd Corps had been well and truly mauled by the divisions of Picton and Leith – 23 out of 27 French infantry battalions involved were broken. But there was no time for Wellington to relax. Soon the sound of artillery and musketry was heard further north and the British Commander galloped towards it.

THE NORTHERN SECTOR

Ney's 6th Corps was now attacking. Ney had spotted General Merle's division briefly on the crest before it was repulsed, and, assuming that Reynier's attack had been successful, ordered his own corps forward. The Marshal threw his men up the steep slopes alongside the road that ran between the villages of Moura and Busacco. He had two divisions – General Louis Henri Loison's on the right of the road and General Jean Gabriel Marchand's on the left – a total force of 23 battalions. Facing them was 'Black' Bob Craufurd's Light Division, including Captain Ross's troop of horse artillery, which soon began blasting away at the approaching French with a deadly barrage of shrapnel shells. Craufurd watched Loison's Division advance, proudly eyeing the superb skirmishing of his rifleman and the Portuguese Caçadores as they picked apart the attacking columns.

Behind Craufurd, hidden out of view of the French, were 1,800 men of his elite 43rd and 52nd Regiments. The French came forward full of confidence, their officers cheering them on and waving their hats on top of swords. The drummers beat the *pas de charge*. To the men in the column, exhausted from the steep climb, it appeared that the day was won. But, as the French closed to within 20 metres, Craufurd turned to the two regiments of light infantry lying behind him and screamed, 'Now 52nd, revenge the death of Sir John Moore!' With a cheer the redcoats rushed forward, fired a devastating volley, and then charged. Lieutenant Charles Booth of the 43rd Regiment picks up the story:

> The front of their columns alone – chiefly composed of officers – stood the charge; the rest took to their heels, throwing away their arms and pouches etc. Our men did not stand to take prisoners; what were taken were those left in our rear. . .The advanced part of the charging line. . .after throwing themselves into the midst of the enemies retreating columns, killing, wounding, and in short felling to the ground lots of them, were with great difficulty halted, and then commenced from the flanks of the whole division the most destructive flanking fire that I believe I ever witnessed.[27]

Amongst the prisoners taken by the Light Division was French General of Brigade Simon. He was captured by Private James Hopkins of the 52^{nd,} who received a pension of £20 per annum for his bravery.[28]

Nearby, Marchand's division suffered a similar fate at the hands of Brigadier General Pack's well-drilled and confident Portuguese troops. The French, when seeing the uniforms of their enemy, had assumed that they would have an easy victory. They were wrong. The heavy Portuguese volley fire stopped them in their tracks and soon forced them to fall back.

Fighting in the French ranks that day was a young German, Johann Maempel, who would later switch sides and join the King's German Legion. His account of the battle indicates the ferocity of the fight and the heavy French casualties:

> Our troops attacked with their usual impetuosity, but were so

warmly received by the riflemen of the German legion, and of the 60th and 95th regiments, that they fell in all directions; every shot told, and our regiment alone had seven officers killed, besides the wounded: in my company there were forty-eight killed and; the captain was shot through the body and was carried to the hospital at Coimbra. . .We attacked the heights at the point of the bayonet; but before we had reached half way, we were driven back with great loss.[29]

By lunchtime, the battle was as good as over. Though defeated, the French had shown tremendous courage and fortitude – attacking uphill against a strong, natural defensive position. But despite their bravery, it was an ill-conceived attack that was never likely to be successful against troops of the calibre of Wellington's redcoats and his excellent Portuguese regiments. Those Portuguese units had well and truly proven themselves as the equal of any soldiers in the Peninsular. The Allied troops had destroyed every French attack sent against them. Line had beaten column once more, and Wellington had proved that he was a master of choosing the best ground and using it superbly.

The French casualties reflected the difficulty of their task – 4,600 killed, wounded or captured, including 300 officers. Allied losses, on the other hand, were around 1,200 – nearly half of them Portuguese.[30]

As his men dug in and bury their dead, Marshal Masséna finally realised his folly. Seeing that another attack was unlikely to end differently, he ordered his cavalry to search for a way to outflank the ridge. Early the next day, they discovered a rough track to the north and soon the French were on the march. With his position now in danger, Wellington, much to the irritation of his soldiers, withdrew. It was time to fall back and give the French yet another surprise. . .the amazing engineering feat that was the *Lines of Torres Vedras*.

CHAPTER THREE: THE LINES OF TORRES VEDRAS

THE RETREAT

The rain fell in lead sheets. The roads, thick with mud, were choked with people. Dead animals and abandoned luggage lay scattered all around. Civilians carrying what little possessions they had rescued swarmed alongside bullock carts filled with wounded soldiers. Everyone was heading to Lisbon. The Portuguese civilians had been ordered to destroy everything they could not carry – but such an order was difficult to enforce and they had inadvertently left behind a large amount of food for the enemy.

As August Schaumann of the King's German Legion remembered:

> A new reign of terror now began for Portugal. Her defenders, driven back by superior forces, had to leave the Mondego, whose fertile banks would be at the mercy of the enemy. But the French had not been expected so soon in these parts. . .The maize harvest had not yet begun. All the fields and many of the barns were full up, and as there was a shortage of carts and mules the poor inhabitants were forced to leave behind everything they could not move, and were only able to save their children, cattle and a few portable treasures. Their flight was carried out partly in pursuance in of orders and partly from instinct; for they knew the French and their lust for murder and plunder, and were only too familiar with the ill-treatment that awaited them.[31]

It was a tough time, both for the civilians and soldiers of the Allied army. John Kincaid, a subaltern with the 1/95th Rifles, remembered the withdrawal after the Battle of Busacco as one of the most trying he ever experienced:

> We were on our legs from daylight until dark, in daily contact with the enemy; and, to satisfy the stomach of an ostrich, I had. . .only a pound of beef, a pound of biscuit, and one glass of rum. A brother-officer was kind enough to strap my boat-cloak and portmanteau on the mule carrying his heavy baggage, which, on account of the proximity of the foe, was never permitted to be

within a day's march of us, so that, in addition to my simple uniform, my only covering every night was the canopy of heaven, from whence the dews descended so refreshingly, that I generally awoke, at the end of an hour, chilled, and wet to the skin; and I could only purchase an equal length of additional repose by jumping up and running about, until I acquired a sleeping quantity of warmth. Nothing in life can be more ridiculous than seeing a lean, lank fellow start from a profound sleep, at midnight, and begin lashing away at the highland fling, as if St. Andrew himself had been playing the bagpipes; but it was a measure that I very often had recourse to, as the cleverest method of producing heat.[32]

By the second week of October, wet and exhausted, the redcoats arrived at the newly built lines of Torres Vedras. The discovery of these defensive works, rising out of the mist above them, was an enormous surprise for most of the army. Lieutenant Charles Leslie of the 29th Regiment of Foot was on a boat, escorting wounded soldiers to Lisbon, when he and the other officers on board caught their first glimpse of the lines:

About a league below Villa Franca we observed a considerable range of heights on the right bank of the Tagus, rising from the town of Alhandra, and stretching towards the west, on which appeared batteries and embankments. I inquired of the boatman what these were. He answered, 'Oh, sir, those are the lines.' This was an enigma to us, but my friend the aide-de-camp solved the mystery. He said, 'That is the position Lord Wellington is now falling back upon, and where he means to meet the enemy.' This threw a new light upon us. Everyone wondered and became animated. Each one seemed to take an intense interest in examining the little we could see of such works as we swept along. It was unanimously agreed that our valiant commander had in this displayed the utmost sagacity. His secret had been well kept. None of us had ever heard of these preparations.[33]

Schaumann, arriving at the town of Alverca, later recalled:

Here we obtained the first glimpse of the fortified lines which Lord Wellington had built upon a chain of hills which seem to have been destined for this purpose by nature herself. Running from Alverca to Peniche on the sea, they encircled Lisbon completely, and had been studded with batteries, mines trenches and barricades. As far as the eye could see there was nothing but gun embrasures. Earthworks on the hill and barricades made with wine casks, boxes and even trunks filled with earth and stones, formed the entrance to Villa Franca; every means of access was blocked. A few 24-pounders frowned darkly on the road. To the left of the Tagus lay a respectable looking fleet of gun boats manned by English sailors. All garden walls had been thrown down and trenches ran to the very edge of the river. As up in the north with the army we had not heard of these prudent measures of defence, our surprise at what we now saw may well be imagined. I sang Lord Wellington's praises.[34]

Construction of the lines had been ongoing for over a year – British and Portuguese Engineering officers, with the help of large numbers of local civilian labourers, had done a tremendous job. The naturally steep hills lining the approach to Lisbon were strengthened, scarped, and entrenched. Over 150 forts and redoubts covered all the important positions, their arcs of fire overlapping and deadly.

And it was not just one line, there were multiple – four in total.[35] The first, which the Allied troops now occupied, stretched for approximately 26 miles from Sizandro to Alhandra. A combination of over 30,000 Portuguese militia, 8,000 Spanish soldiers under General Don Pedro La Romana, and 2,500 British sailors and marines manned the forts and redoubts.[36] Wellington did not want his regular British and Portuguese divisions tied down behind defensive works. He needed his best troops to be free to manoeuvre and meet the French wherever they might attack.

Despite reaching the lines, life for the infantry did not immediately become easier, as Charles Leslie relates:

I had got a billet on a house, the inmates of which, in common with their neighbours, had fled. Not a living creature, dog or cat, was remaining in it, only myself and my servant. Wearied with my long march that morning and weakened with fever, I had just got some tea and was taking off my coat to lie down on a mattress, about eight o'clock, when the alarm was given. An orderly announced that the troops were instantly to get under arms. In

31

an amazing short time, each brigade was formed in its respective position. We were then marched out of the town, up to the heights, and formed in contiguous close column of battle in rear of the lines which ran from the plain to the west, while the light troops were posted at the entrance in front of the town, and the wet ditches running from the town across a narrow piece of flat ground to the Tagus. Whilst waiting in this order it became pitch-dark, piercingly cold, with incessant showers of heavy rain. There we were obliged to stand, up to the ankles in mud, wet to the skin, sleepy as death, no chance of getting under cover, no possibility of sitting down, not allowed even to move about to keep up a little warmth during the pelting storm of this wretched night. I must confess my resolution was never more severely tried than on this occasion. The long-looked-for daylight at length appeared, and the enemy not having dashed on as was expected, patrols were sent out from the town, who on their return reported that the enemy's advanced posts were established about a mile in front.[37]

THE BATTLE OF SOBRAL, 14th OF OCTOBER 1810.

Marshal Masséna was stunned when he saw the extent of the Allied entrenchments and realised that his easy entry into Lisbon had been denied. His intelligence assets had let him down and now he had to decide – should he order a swift and decisive assault, dig in, or withdraw?

On the 14th of October, the Marshal probed the Allied positions around the town of Sobral, 21 miles north of Lisbon. General Jean-Andoche Junot's 8th Corps was tasked with the mission. Ensign Andrew Leith-Hay of the 1/29th witnessed the action:

The morning was cloudless, succeeded by a day of bright sunshine. Encouraged by these appearances, and curious to observe the position of the enemy, accompanied by Lord George Grenville, I rode to the advanced posts. We left our horses in the ravine which separated the heights, on which was the position of the Allied army, from a rising ground where a breastwork had been thrown up to protect a post occupied by part of the 71st Regiment, and about one hundred and fifty yards removed from which was a French work, constructed of casks, doors, and planks, brought from Sobral. Behind this the enemy's infantry were perceived, but apparently quiet. For some time, we continued to observe the different detachments more immediately opposite. Between the breast-work and the temporary redoubt of the enemy, extended a level field, on which neither a tree nor obstruction of any description presented itself. The French soldiers were observed looking from behind the casks, but not a shot was fired by either party. Our attention was soon after attracted to the road leading from Alenquer into the town of Sobral. A crowd of officers on horseback, detachments of cavalry, dragoons with led horses, and all the cortege of a general-in-chief, appeared upon it. The drums beat; the troops in rear of the village got under arms: still no movement was perceptible in the post to which we were immediately opposed. It was, however, evident that a reconnaissance of some importance was contemplated; nor did it appear probable the troops would be permitted long to continue in their present inactive state. Marshal Masséna, the Duke d'Elchingen, and General Junot, ascended to a height a short distance to the north of the town, where they dismounted, near a windmill, and became seated, apparently reconnoitring the position opposite. Soon after their arrival, a rocket was fired from the cask redoubt, succeeded by the unmasking of some light guns, which were instantaneously discharged against the breastwork of the 71st. We had previously been kneeling, looking over the embankment, which was struck near its crest by the shot fired. The British detachment continued protected until after the first musketry discharge of the enemy, on receiving which, the men started up, making a deadly return to the comparatively harmless volley. The French infantry, after this preamble, rushed forward with their usual impetuosity, reaching the embankment unchecked, when the 71st, with Colonel Reynell at their head, springing over the work, not only bayoneted the enemy back to his intrenchment, but drove him from thence into the town.[38]

Amongst the defenders was Thomas Pococke, from Glasgow, and his colleagues of the 71st (Highland) Regiment of Foot:

We were scarce able to withstand their fury. To retreat was impossible; all behind being ploughed land, rendered deep by the rain. There was not a moment to hesitate. To it we fell, pell-mell,

French and British mixed together. It was a trial of strength in single combat; every man had his opponent, many had two. I got one up to the wall, on the point of my bayonet. He was unhurt: I would have spared him: but he would not spare himself. He cursed and defied me, nor ceased to attack my life, until he fell, pierced by my bayonet. His breath died away in a curse and menace. This was the work of a moment: I was compelled to this extremity. I was again attacked, but my antagonist fell, pierced by a random shot. We soon forced them to retire over the wall, cursing their mistake. At this moment; I stood gasping for breath; not a shoe on my feet: my bonnet had fallen to the ground. Unmindful of my situation, I followed the enemy over the wall. We pursued them about a mile, and then fell back to the wane of our struggle.[39]

The battle was over almost as soon as it began. It had been a half-hearted assault by the French infantry. Masséna, realising the futility of reinforcing failure, halted the attack. It was a sensible decision, but many British officers considered it a mistake not to try and force a passage through their lines:

We have since kicked the French out of more formidable-looking and stronger places; and, with all due deference be it spoken, I think that the Prince of Essling ought to have tried his luck against them, as he could only have been beaten by fighting, as he afterwards was without it! And if he thinks that he would have lost as many men by trying, as he did by not trying, he must allow me to differ in opinion with him!![40]

Moyle Sherer, of the 2/34th, had similar sentiments:

I am more and more astonished that Masséna never attempted to force our position. . .I shall ever be of the opinion that if the enemy had determined to sacrifice everything to the grand objective of penetrating our line, and marching on Lisbon, they might very possibly have effected their purpose. . .We should have been more particularly liable to such a misfortune, in the hurry of the two or three first days after we entered the lines, and before the grammar of their defence was thoroughly understood by all our generals.[41]

The Allied army now waited patiently. Sergeant John Spencer

Cooper of the 2/7th Royal Fusiliers remembered:

> Though we were not allowed during these wearisome six weeks to strip off either belts or clothes, yet cleanliness was insisted upon. Every regiment was also required to be on its respective parade ground an hour before daylight, in full marching order. To strengthen the already impregnable redoubts, etc., working parties were sent daily to handle the pick and shovel on the mountain tops and sides.[42]

The weather was indeed atrocious. Heavy rains poured relentlessly down on the men in the lines, creating miserable, sleepless conditions for the soldiers. William Grattan would later reminisce about how he and the men of the 88th spent their nights smoking cigars and drinking brandy. However, despite the hardship, morale held strong. He recalled that:

> [We were] waiting for the signal to proceed to our alarm-post, a duty which the army performed every morning two hours before day. This was by no means a pleasant task; scrambling up a hill of mud and standing shivering for a couple of hours in the dark and wet was exceedingly uncomfortable, but I don't remember to have heard one single murmur; we all saw the necessity of such a line of conduct, and we obeyed it with cheerfulness.

THE FRENCH WITHDRAW

In their waterlogged bivouacs on the other side of no-man's-land, the French suffered. Their supply lines were over-stretched and the Portuguese guerrillas made foraging for food a difficult and dangerous operation. Thomas Pococke described an amusing encounter with the desperately hungry enemy:

> The advanced picquet of the French lay in a windmill ours, consisting of one captain, two subalterns, and 400 men, in a small village. There was only a distance of about 150 yards between us. We learned from the deserters, that the French were much in want of provisions. To provoke them, our sentinels, at times, would fix a biscuit to the point of their bayonets, and present to

them. One day the French had a bullock, in endeavouring to kill which, their butcher missed his blow, and the animal ran off right into our lines. The French looked so foolish, we hurried at them, secured the bullock, brought him in front, killed him in style. They looked on, but dared not approach to seize him. Shortly after, an officer and four men came with a flag of truce, and supplicated in the most humble manner for the half of the bullock, which they got for godsake.[43]

Exhausted and emaciated French soldiers were beginning to desert to the British in considerable numbers. But judging by Wellington's General Order to the army dated the 10th of November 1810, British troops were also crossing in the opposite direction:

The Commander of the Forces is concerned to have received reports from some of the regiments of the desertion of British soldiers to the enemy; a crime which in all his experience in the British service, in different parts of the world, was till lately unknown in it; and the existence of which, at the present moment, he can attribute only to some false hopes held out to these unfortunate criminal persons. The British soldiers cannot but be aware of the difference between their situation and that of the enemy opposed to them; and the miserable tale told by the half-starved wretches whom they see daily coming into their lines ought alone, exclusive to their sense of honour and patriotism, to be sufficient to deter them from participating in their miserable fate.[44]

Many of Wellington's officers felt that the poor condition of the French army presented them with the perfect time to attack, but Wellington was playing the long game. His strategy was working, and it required patience to see it through. It's true that a decisive victory would have helped relieve the political pressure on Wellington but he remained focused, 'I could lick those fellows any day,' he said, 'but it would cost me 10,000 men and, as this is the last army England has got, we must take care of it.'[45] He had the foresight to see that a failed attack with heavy casualties would likely result in the politicians in London ordering the army to return to Britain.

In the dark, on the early morning of the 15th of November, Marshal Masséna's Army of Portugal finally withdrew. Jonathan

Leach, a very experienced officer of the 95th Rifles, recalled:

> I happened to be on picket in front of Arruda on the night of the 14th; and looking as usual, with all our eyes in the twilight of the following morning, towards our opponents, the French sentries, we thought, could be discovered as heretofore: but when day broke thoroughly, we found that the cunning rogues had played us an old trick of theirs, by placing figures of straw upright, with a soldiers cap on each and a pole by their side to represent a musket. Their whole army had retired, during the night, in the direction of Santarem; and we were sent in pursuit some hours afterwards. [46]

Masséna pulled his force 30 miles north to the town of Santarem, where the hills and surrounding marshes offered them a strong defensive position. He then ordered his men to dig in and prepare to hold their ground. Masséna hoped the region would yield more food for his famished soldiers and that reinforcements would soon reach him. The Marshal also wanted the British to attack and bleed themselves dry against his own strong defences. But, as before, Wellington refused to oblige.

The campaign of 1810 was now over. The two armies settled down opposite one another and played a waiting game. The British would spend the next few months trying to remain active and blocking the increasingly desperate French attempts to forage for food. However, Masséna's men, used to living off the land, were skilled in the art of finding hidden supplies. Cavalry officer William Tomkinson recalled:

> The enemy have become so expert at finding where the inhabitants hide their grain that they flood all around the houses (where it is possible), and then dig where the water sinks, which it generally does where the corn is buried. They likewise measure the outside of the house, and if the inside measure does not correspond with the outside they are satisfied (on its being less) that there is some secret hiding-place within, which throughout Portugal is very common. From the system of their own government, and exorbitant demands of the priests, they have always some secret hiding-place for grain, wine, oil, etc.[47]

Despite these tricks, Masséna's men continued to suffer from extreme hunger. Inevitably, the soldiers of both sides, cold and bored, fraternised. A friendly relationship developed between opposing pickets, Schaumann remembered:

> Before dinner we often rode to a small river where our outpost was stationed. Across this river there was a bridge which was barricaded. On the opposite bank stood the French sentries. . .On these occasions the French officers would come down and have a chat with us. *'Bonjour, messieurs,'* was the salutation from either bank. They admired our beautiful English horses, spoke of our good King George. . .they also sang the praises of Lord Wellington and the Portuguese troops. They told us that they had a theatre in Santarem at which every night a piece entitled 'The Entry of the French into Lisbon' was acted. We retorted smartly that very soon they would act the piece called 'The Flight of the French,' at which they all laughed. We also gave them all the news and they would throw their water bottles over to us to be filled with wine, and we would exchange our English newspapers for their French ones.[48]

Subaltern John Kincaid, of the Rifles, remembered that the 'live and let live' attitude between the advanced posts surprised visitors to the front:

> Our piquet-post, at the bridge, became a regular lounge, for the winter, to all manner of folks. I used to be much amused at seeing our naval officers come up from Lisbon riding on mules, with huge ships' spy-glasses, like six-pounders, strapped across the backs of their saddles. Their first question invariably was, 'Who is that fellow there?' (Pointing to the enemy's sentry, close to us), and, on being told that he was a Frenchman, 'Then why the devil don't you shoot him!' Repeated acts of civility passed between the French and us during this tacit suspension of hostilities. The greyhounds of an officer followed a hare, on one occasion, into their lines, and they very politely returned them. I was one night on piquet, at the end of the bridge, when a ball came from the French sentry and struck the burning billet of wood round which we were sitting, and they sent in a flag of truce, next morning, to apologise for the accident, and to say that it had been done by a stupid fellow of a sentry, who imagined that people were

advancing upon him. We admitted the apology, though we knew well enough that it had been done by a malicious rather than a stupid fellow, from the situation we occupied.[49]

During the winter of 1810-1811, the ability of the French to live off the land astonished Wellington. Somehow, against the odds, they survived and held their ground. But the cost was devastating – the strength of Masséna's army fell from around 65,000 at the start of the invasion to just 45,000.[50] Those that remained were weak and desperate.

In February 1811, with reinforcements and supplies unable to reach him, Masséna called his senior officers together for a council of war. They decided that a retreat was the only viable option for the ailing army. Johann Maempel, serving with the French, later wrote:

> The small remaining stock of provisions was divided, each man receiving thirteen biscuits; the baggage, and the sick and wounded, owing to the want of horses, were left behind, and everything got in readiness for the march. The army was in a miserable condition; without clothes, without shoes, without provisions, and reduced one-half in numbers, was on the point of commencing a retreat through a devastated country with roads in the worst possible condition, and pressed on all sides by an enemy eager for battle, and provided with every requisite.[51]

RETREAT

During the early morning of the 6th of March, the French left their redoubts and retreated. Once again, straw dummies dressed in shakos and armed with broom sticks fooled the British pickets for some hours until the early morning fog lifted. The French, aware of how exposed they would be once they left the safety of Santarem, moved fast – leaving a trail of abandoned wagons and hamstrung animals. Along the way, they blew the bridges at Alviela and Pernes, determined to put as much space as they could between themselves and the pursuing Allies. The timing of the French retreat was unfortunate for Wellington, who had recently been reinforced by

Major General John Houston's 7th Division and was preparing to launch his own offensive.

On the 11th of March, the French rear-guard under Marshal Ney turned on the advancing Allies and repulsed a badly coordinated attack on the heights behind the town of Pombal. It was the first of several such actions fought by Ney during the next few days that would save the rest of the Army of Portugal from being caught and destroyed by the British.

Sergeant John Spencer Cooper of the 2/7th Fusiliers recalled a fight near the village of Redhina, on the 12th of March:

> After skirmishing in a wood on our left, we debouched into the open plain, and prepared to attack. 'Form close column'; 'prime and load'; 'fix bayonets'; 'shoulder'; 'slope'; 'silence'; 'steady'; 'deploy into line'; 'forward.' We moved across the plain in three or four parallel lines towards the French batteries, which now opened upon us briskly. This was immediately followed by as heavy a fire of musketry as I ever heard in the Peninsula. The balls flew from both combatants like hail. But this duel did not last long; the enemy gave way, and carried off their artillery at a rattling pace, followed by loud English hurrahs, and our skirmishers. We hurried through the burning village to overtake them; but they waded the river, and made good use of their legs. Marshal Ney commanded the retreat, and did it well, so that few prisoners were taken.[52]

At Foz de Arouce, on the 15th of March, Ney found himself with his back against the River Ceira. There was only one narrow bridge over which they could cross the rocky, swollen river – a similar situation to that faced by Craufurd's Light Division outside Almeida the previous July.

When the British 3rd and Light Divisions attacked in the late afternoon, Ney's men panicked and were nearly routed, as Jonathan Leach observed:

> At length they [the French] were forced back in utter confusion, on the narrow bridge, which their comrades on the opposite side blew up; thus, leaving on the same side of the river with the British, many of their countrymen, who were drowned in the

Ceira, by attempting to flounder through its rapid stream. Some hundreds perished in this manner; and they threw two of their eagles into the river, to prevent them becoming trophies of the victors.[53]

Crossing the river two days later, August Schaumann was witness to the grisly aftermath:

The banks were still covered with dead bodies. A number of exhausted donkeys, horses and mules, which had not been able to wade across the large smooth stones of the roaring stream, and which the barbarians had made unfit for use by either hamstringing them or twisting their necks, were still writhing in the mud, half dead. Among them lay commissariat carts, dead soldiers, women and children, who had died either from want and cold or through the explosion [when the French blew it up]. Over the whole of this ghastly confusion of bodies, our cavalry and artillery now proceeded to march without mercy, until the whole was churned into a mess of blood and slush. Never during the whole of the war did I again see such a horrible site.[54]

Masséna's route to the Spanish border was through a wasteland that offered little food for his starving, broken army. Maempel wrote:

Many a soldier in the first two days had consumed his scanty allowance, and found himself obliged, if he did not choose to die of hunger, to procure himself provisions by whatever means lay in his power. No one could assist his comrade, because no one possessed anything. The soldiers were compelled to plunder, and this occasioned the greatest disorder on the march: whole companies left the main body, and did not rejoin it until their arrival on the Spanish frontier. . .Many returned with booty, in addition to their provisions; but many owing to their thirst for plunder, as the gratification of their unbridled appetites, fell victims to the revenge of the Portuguese peasantry: woe to him who fell into their hands; if innocent, he was sure to suffer for the deeds of the others.[55]

And those deeds had certainly been horrific. British memoirs are peppered with accounts of French brutality against the Portuguese civilians. John Kincaid wrote in his diary:

> We found the body of a well-dressed female, whom they had murdered by a horrible refinement in cruelty. She had been placed upon her back, alive, in the middle of the street, with the fragment of a rock upon her breast, which it required four of our men to remove.[56]

Schaumann also recalled:

> Murdered peasants lay in all directions. At one place, which contained some fine buildings, I halted at a door to beg water of a man who was sitting on the threshold of the house staring fixedly before him. He proved to be dead, and had only been placed there, as if he was still alive, for a joke. The inside of the house was ghastly to behold. All its inmates lay murdered in their beds, but their faces were so peaceful that they looked as if they were sleeping, and some were even smiling. They had probably been surprised at night by the French advanced guard and murdered. The corpse of another Portuguese peasant had been placed in a ludicrous position in a hole in a garden wall through which the infantry had broken. It had probably been put there in order to make fun of us when we came along.[57]

THE BATTLE OF SABUGAL, 3rd OF APRIL 1811

On the 3rd of April, Wellington caught up with General Jean Reynier's 2nd Corps (comprising three divisions) that had lingered too long on the far bank of the Coa River. Wellington's plan was for his 3rd, 5th and 7th Divisions to attack the French in front of the town while the Light Division and two cavalry brigades under the command of Major General William Erskine[58] initiated a flanking movement to the south. The fog was so thick that most of the units did not attack as scheduled, and Lieutenant Colonel Thomas Sydney Beckwith's 1st Brigade of the Light Division waded unsupported across the river to attack an enemy force of around 12,000 men.

John Kincaid, of the Rifles, was in the thick of the action and gives a sense of the confusion:

> Early this morning our division moved still farther to its right, and our brigade led the way across a ford, which took us up to the

middle; while the balls from the enemy's advanced post were hissing in the water around us, we drove in their light troops and commenced a furious assault upon their main body. Thus far all was right; but a thick drizzling rain now came on, in consequence of which the third division, which was to have made a simultaneous attack to our left, missed their way, and a brigade of dragoons under Sir William Erskine, who were to have covered our right, went the Lord knows where, but certainly not into the fight, although they started at the same time that we did, and had the music of our rifles to guide them; and, even the second brigade of our own division could not afford us any support, for nearly an hour, so that we were thus unconsciously left with about fifteen hundred men, in the very impertinent attempt to carry a formidable position, on which stood as many thousands.[59]

Captain James Ferguson of the 43rd Regiment of Foot, which had crossed the river alongside the Rifles, remembered:

We had been scarcely formed when the riflemen were driven in and passed silently through our line; immediately two strong columns of the enemy approached. . .The 43rd Regiment stood alone to defend the ground; our 2nd Brigade not having yet passed the river, the whole of whole Regnier's [sic] Corps being in our immediate front, but the fog prevented our relative situations from being seen. Immediately, with a British cheer, we charged, routed the columns and threw them back in confusion on the main body. Having gained the low ground in our charge, we discovered the enemy's main body strongly posted above, and cautiously retiring to our original ground, had scarcely gained it when three fresh columns of greater strength again advanced against us. The fog at this time in a degree clearing away, we discovered a wall in our front lined by a battalion of the enemy, with a howitzer in the rear that had been dealing destruction in our ranks. We remained firm and steady under a heavy fire of grape and musketry until the enemy's columns neared us, when we again charged, routed, and drove them from the wall, taking the howitzer.[60]

At this moment, the 2/52nd deployed to the right of Ferguson and his company. With the rain falling heavily, the British continued the advance until the French, reinforced by cavalry, emerged from the treeline, and stormed forward. French drummers beat the *pas de charge* while the green-coated dragoons in their impressive brass helmets, poured forward, charging amongst the British infantry and causing momentary panic amongst the 52nd. Luckily, the 52nd were a tough, battle-hardened outfit containing men like Private Patrick Lowe. The history of the regiment recalls that as the men fell back, Private Lowe was too slow to keep up and was nearly overtaken by a French cavalryman:

> Finding that he had no time to get back to the walls behind which the greater part of his comrades were now making cover, he took refuge behind an old stump of a tree; came to the right about; down on one knee, and deliberately covered the trooper with his piece, and the butt to his cheek. The dragoon at once reined up, and not liking the look of either Pat, or his muzzle, began to curvet right and left, hoping to induce him to throw away his fire. Lowe, however, remained steady as a rock, and as cool as on parade, still covering his man. Some of his comrades from the wall wished to bring down the dragoon, but were stopped by the others, who called out that he was Pat's lawful game, and ought not to be taken away from him. Almost immediately the regiment in perfect order advanced and to the surprise of everyone Lowe allowed his friend to ride off unharmed. When he was roundly taxed by the leading officer for such conduct, as 'being a fool not to shoot him,' the reply was irresistible. 'Is it shooting you mane, Sir? Sure, how could I shoot him when I wasn't loaded.' [61]

Lieutenant Colonel Beckwith's heavily outnumbered brigade had somehow survived the bitter and confusing fight and now, supported by the 2nd Brigade of the Light Division, they stormed forward to carry the French position at the top of the ridge. Beckwith had been instrumental in the brigade's defiant and surprising success – with blood streaming down his face, he bravely rode up and down his lines, roaring encouragement to the men. Wellington later wrote, 'the action fought by the Light Division with the whole of the 2nd Corps, to be one of the most glorious that British troops were ever engaged in.'

Meanwhile, General Picton's 3rd Division finally joined the fight. Amongst them was Private Joseph Donaldson of the 94th:

When we gained the edge of the river, the French columns were posted on the heights above us. We passed the river under a heavy fire, and proceeded to ascend the hill. We could now see that more of our army had crossed, both to our right and left. As we advanced up the hill we formed line. General Picton rode up in front of us, with his stick over his shoulder, exposed to the heavy fire of the enemy, as composedly as if he had been in perfect safety. 'Steady my lads, steady!' said he; 'don't throw away your fire until I give you the word of command.' We were now close on them; the balls were whizzing about our ears like hailstones. The man before me received a shot in the head and fell. 'Why don't they let us give the rascals a volley?' said some of the men. The left of our brigade, which was nearest them, now opened a heavy fire; and by the time the line was all formed, the French had taken to their heels.[62]

The French were now in full flight. Masséna's only option was to fall back across the border to Spain. Within days, the only formed body of French troops remaining in Portugal was the small garrison of Almeida.

Wellington had achieved his aim – the third French invasion of Portugal had been contained and then forced to retreat. It had been a spectacular victory for the Allied army. But it was a different type of victory – one won not just on the field of battle but through Wellington's long-term strategic vision, the hard work of his engineers and labourers, the incredible sacrifice of the Portuguese population, and what the historian Charles Oman calls 'the sword of famine.'

CHAPTER FOUR: THE BATTLE OF BAROSSA

As Wellington pushed the French from Portugal, British and Portuguese troops were also engaged in another theatre of the Peninsular War.

The Spanish city of Cadiz sits on the Atlantic Ocean. It is a beautiful city full of charming 18th century watch towers that rise above the atmospheric, white-washed narrow streets. During the French Revolutionary and Napoleonic wars, it was the principal home port of the Spanish navy. By 1810, following the French occupation of Madrid and Seville, it had also become the seat of the Spanish government – known as the Cortes of Cadiz.

As the French divisions under Marshals Claude Victor and Jean de Dieu Soult advanced deeper into Andalucía, the Spanish were quickly surrounded and besieged in the city. At first, the Spanish commanders rejected the possibility of British help. After all, Spain had been at war with Britain only a few years before and they were still resentful of the British control of Gibraltar. But eventually, realising that losing Cadiz would be disastrous, the Spanish government relented, and a small British force was dispatched from Lisbon in February 1810.

In March, the redcoat reinforcements arrived along with a new commanding officer – Lieutenant General Sir Thomas Graham. Graham was a Scottish laird who had quit the peaceful life of a landowning gentleman to fight the French after the death of his wife. In 1792, she had died on a boat off the south of France. While escorting her body home for burial, Graham was accosted by French revolutionaries who opened the coffin and disturbed her body. Angered and upset, he dedicated his life to fighting the French – volunteering for action at the siege of Toulon and then raising the 90th Regiment of Foot (Perthshire Volunteers). Over the succeeding years, he saw action during the siege of Malta, served in the West Indies and was alongside Sir John Moore during the arduous retreat to Corunna. It was an impressive C.V. for a soldier who hadn't donned a uniform until he was in his forties.

Once he reached the front lines in Cadiz, Lieutenant General Graham, like Wellington, soon came to understand the difficulties of working alongside the Spanish – though they needed British help, they were often jealous and suspicious. The Spanish rank and file were brave and proud, but they lacked strong leadership and were poorly equipped. Many of the Spanish soldiers hadn't been paid for a long time, and the commanders in Cadiz had made no effort to recruit and train the local populace. Quarter-master Sergeant William Surtees, with the 95th Rifles, later wrote of the Spanish soldiers in Cadiz:

> While here, I had a most ample opportunity of closely viewing the Spanish army, great numbers being stationed in and about the Isla, and great numbers constantly coming into and going out of the place, after receiving such equipment as the government was able to provide for them. Nothing could exceed the hardy and robust appearance of the men in general; and had they been clothed, appointed, and disciplined like either their enemies or their allies, there could not have been a finer soldiery. I cannot, however, say so much for their officers; most of them appeared to be utterly unfit and unable to command their men. Those who had the means, seemed to think of nothing else but dressing like apes or mountebanks, and intriguing with the women. It was really absurd and ludicrous to see the strange figures they generally made themselves. In one regiment alone you might have observed more different uniforms than both we and the French have in all our armies. One would have had on a blue coat turned up with red, with a chaco [sic] and a straight sword, the uniform prescribed for officers of the infantry, I believe; the next would have most likely had on a hussar dress, with an enormous sabre dangling by his side; another would have had a red coat, a fourth yellow, a fifth white, and so on. In short, all the colours of the rainbow were generally exhibited in the uniforms of one regiment's officers; and every one of them appeared to vie with the other who could make the greatest harlequin of himself, whilst those of them who were mounted would caper and prance about the streets like so many fools, riding with their legs at full stretch, and the toe of the boot (if they had one) just touching the stirrup, and drawing the reins continually through the fingers of their right hand; and if by any chance an ape of this kind came

near the window of his dulcinea, and thought there was a likelihood of her seeing him, I pitied the poor foot-passengers who might happen to be near him, for he would make his unfortunate Rosinante prance and caper by the immense long bit in its mouth, and the pieces of iron in the shape of spurs on his (shoes perhaps), till the poor animal was like to fall under him. In short, they had all the pride, arrogance, and self-sufficiency of the best officers in the world, with the very least of all pretension to have a high opinion of themselves; it is true they were not all alike, but the majority of them were the most haughty, and at the same time the most contemptible creatures in the shape of officers, that I ever beheld. It was, therefore, not to be expected that the soldiers would or could look upon them with that degree of respect and reverence so essential to a due maintenance of subordination in an army.[63]

Lieutenant General Graham's force was a strong one. It included two composite battalions of the Foot Guards as well as the 2/47th, 2/67th, 2/87th, a half battalion of the 2/95th and two battalions of the 20th Portuguese Line Regiment. There were also two squadrons of the 2nd Hussars of the King's German Legion, and two artillery batteries.

The British priority was to stop the French from overrunning the city and the redcoats spent much of their time working to improve the city's defences. But when Marshal Soult had marched north to attack Badajoz in January 1811, the Allies saw an opportunity to raise the siege of Cadiz and defeat the army of Marshal Victor.

To maintain good relations with the Spanish, Graham agreed to serve as a subordinate to the Spanish Commander-in-Chief, General Manuel La Peña. Sadly, La Peña was a poor soldier of limited ability and frayed nerves – even his own men had nicknamed him *'Lady Manuela'* because of his unwillingness to meet the French in battle.

THE EXPEDITION SETS SAIL

On February 21st, 1811, the expedition set sail from Cadiz. The plan was to land nearly 14,000 men (over 4,000 of them British) on the coast near Tarifa. From there, the army would march back towards Cadiz and attack the French in the rear. It was a risky operation. If things were to go wrong, and the force found itself exposed and beaten in open battle, then there was a very good chance that Cadiz would fall shortly afterwards – a situation that would be a disaster for the Allies.

Things didn't start well. Due to bad weather, the troop ships couldn't land at Tarifa. Instead, they had to disembark the army further along the coast, at Algeciras. The troops then marched back to Tarifa and joined a composite battalion sent from the British base at Gibraltar, under the command of Lieutenant Colonel John Frederick Browne. This unit comprised several companies from the 1/28th Regiment of Foot and the Light and Grenadier companies of the 1/9th and 2/82nd Regiments.

With so many officers together at Tarifa, Lieutenant Robert Blakeney of the 28th Regiment of Foot would later describe a particularly wild night in the officer's mess:

> The night of the 27th being the last jovial one the army were to pass at Tarifa, one hundred and ninety-one officers dined at the mess. The exhilarating juice of the grape was freely quaffed from out the crystal cup, and the inspiring songs of love and war went joyfully round, and the conclusion of each animating strophe was loudly hailed with choral cheers; for such is the composition of a soldier that the object of his love and his country's foe alike call forth the strongest and most indomitable effusions of his heart, so closely allied is love to battle. Hilarity and mirth reigned throughout. Lively sallies of wit cheerfully received as guilelessly shot forth added brilliancy to the festive board. Officers having entered their profession young, mutual attachment was firmly cemented, genuine and disinterested. Each man felt sure that he sat between two friends; worldly considerations, beyond legitimate pleasures and professional ambition, were banished from our thoughts. The field of glory was present to our view and equally open to all; none meanly envied the proud distinctions which chance of war fortunately threw in the way of others. Our revels continued until the morning; and in the morning, while many a Spanish fair with waving hands and glistening eyes was seen in the balcony, we marched out of Tarifa with aching heads

but glowing hearts.[64]

The Allied force now began an exhausting and farcical series of marches towards Cadiz. The British infantry, along with two attached Spanish regiments, formed the reserve and marched at the rear of the column. Local Spanish guides were useless, and General La Peña's penchant for night marches meant that becoming lost and exhausted was a certainty. Lieutenant General Graham wrote in his diary:

> March 1st: Marched in the evening – very tedious from filing across water and other difficulties. Misled by the guides. . .and counter-marching made a most fatiguing march. . .It was 12 o'clock before the troops halted, having been nineteen hours under arms.[65]

The entire Allied purpose was to draw the French away from Cadiz and relieve the siege. But it seems La Peña soon forgot his original intent, and instead became uncertain and unwilling to fight. Along the march, he discovered that the town of Medina Sidonia was garrisoned by a large French force, which if attacked, would force French Marshal Claude Victor to send reserves and likely result in a decisive battle. But, La Peña, true to form, decided against this course of action. Instead, he turned the column around and began marching back towards the coast. La Peña then chose a poor road for the column to follow. It was flooded with choppy water, whipped up by a heavy wind – the only way across was via a narrow causeway that was also submerged. The Spanish, at the front of the column, removed their footwear and gingerly made their way across in single-file – the officers ordering their men to carry them on their shoulders. Graham, realising that this would take all day, rushed forward and advanced into the water, ordering his men to follow him. Sergeant William Surtees was present and recalled:

> My battalion led the van and were ordered to march straight through it without any picking of steps, and to go forward in regular sections, one man supporting another. They went in and marched right through it, as if it had been plain ground, the water

taking them generally about mid-deep. The rest of the British army followed and were all through in less than half an hour; a one-horse cart, indeed, stuck fast in the middle of it, from the wheels having got entangled between the large stones at the bottom. General Graham seeing this, instantly dismounted, and, plunging in, set his shoulder to the wheel, and fairly lifted it clear of the obstruction. La Peña, and those about him, after witnessing the example set them by our General and his troops, seemed really ashamed of their former conduct, and, setting to in good earnest, they contrived to urge their soldiers and officers to take the water with more freedom, and before dark the whole army had got over.[66]

After another long day of marching, the wet and exhausted men finally reached the town of Vejer at midnight. Bizarrely, La Peña was keen to carry on and keep the men on their feet, but Graham, exasperated by the treatment of the soldiers, convinced the Spaniard that the troops needed to rest if they were to meet the French in battle.

Meanwhile, French Marshal Victor was busy making his own plans. He ordered three divisions (the 1st Division under General Francois Ruffin, the 2nd commanded by General Jean Francois Leval and the 3rd under General Eugéne-Casimir Villatte) towards La Peña's column with a plan to block the Allied army and then hit the strung-out column in the flank. The Allied expedition was now in serious danger.

The next day, March 4th, the Allied force left Vejer and commenced another confusing and fatiguing march that lasted throughout the night. The entire army became lost in the darkness, and the Spanish guides almost led them directly into the French camp at Chiclana, on the edge of Cadiz. As Graham wrote:

After some rather ludicrous scenes of distress, several people of the country agreeing that a path to the left led through the heath towards Santi-Petri, and that, the country being dry, the guns could move in all directions over the plain, it was agreed that the march should be continued as I had originally recommended, by a flank movement left in front, forming columns of lines, the cavalry and rear guard on the right in the first line and so on. Our columns closed up, and the army proceeded in this way across the extensive heathy plain of Chiclana, making a remarkably pretty field-day. Our advanced cavalry got upon the Barrosa heights without meeting with any enemy.[67]

Graham and his force occupied the Barrosa heights. It was clearly the dominant feature in the area, rising about 60 meters above sea level, and would need to be held in the event of a French attack. On the summit of the ridge was a tall watch tower and much of the ground in the vicinity was covered with pine woods. Shortly after the redcoats arrived on the ridge, General La Peña requested the British evacuate it and move northwards to protect the Spanish lines of communication. General La Peña's leading elements had just fought a sharp skirmish with the French at the Sancti Petri River, on the edge of Cadiz, and he now wanted to concentrate his force in the event of further fighting. General Graham was loath to give up the ridge that he rightly considered was the key terrain feature in the area. Around midday, Graham finally agreed to vacate the ridge, but he left a strong rearguard behind including two Spanish regiments, Lieutenant Colonel John Frederick Browne's Flank Battalion and a cavalry force under the command of Brigadier General Whittingham – a British officer attached to the Spanish. They were to wait until the rest of Graham's force had redeployed safely and then follow them.

THE FRENCH ATTACK, 5TH OF MARCH 1811

Marshal Claude Victor, a tough, experienced campaigner, seized the moment and ordered the French divisions to attack. As the blue-coated enemy emerged from the woods, the Spanish infantry, who had been placed on the Barossa heights by Lieutenant General Graham, disregarded the threat in front of them, and fell back in retreat. Lieutenant Robert Blakeney, who was serving with the Flank Battalion, picks up the story:

By this time the greater part of the Spanish troops had passed between us and the coast road and were soon in rapid march towards the beach leading to Bermeja. Colonel Browne strongly and rather indignantly remonstrated against their conduct. At this period Colonel [sic] Whittingham rode up, and addressing Colonel Browne said, 'Colonel Browne, what do you intend to do?' The reply was, 'What do I intend to do, sir? I intend to fight the French.' Whittingham then remarked, 'You may do as you please. Colonel Browne, but we are decided on a retreat.' 'Very well, sir,' replied Browne, 'I shall stop where I am, for it shall never be said that John Frederick Browne ran away from the post which his general ordered him to defend.' Generals Murgeon and Beguines were present during the conversation, and as they expressed a wish to know its exact import, I informed them word for word in plain Spanish, which I pledge myself was a correct and full interpretation and could not be misunderstood. Colonel Whittingham again addressed Colonel Browne, saying, 'If you will not come with us but wish to retire on General Graham's division, I shall give you a squadron of cavalry to cover your retreat.' Browne wheeled round, making no answer; and thus a formidable corps, composed of two regiments of Royal Spanish Guards, three regiments of the line, a park of artillery and a strong force of cavalry, all well-armed clad and appointed, undaunted by the scowling frowns of their allies and the reproachful taunts of their own countrymen, were not afraid to run away. They retrograded with firm tread; nor faltering step nor slow was seen, and not one longing lingering look was cast behind. They left four hundred and seventy British bayonets bristling on the neck of the boar.[68]

Lieutenant Colonel Browne ordered the look-out tower to be occupied and loop-holed but soon it became clear that an entire French division supported by cavalry and artillery would quickly engulf his small battalion. He therefore decided, despite his words to Whittingham, his only option was to retire to the foot of the hill.

As they reached the bottom of the slopes, Lieutenant General Graham emerged from the woods. 'Browne,' he called, 'did I not give you orders to defend Barossa hill?'

Browne quickly explained how the premature retreat of the Spanish forces had left him in an exposed position. Graham, realising the perilous situation that the entire Allied force now faced, saw that he had to act decisively. 'it's a bad business, Browne,' he said, 'you must instantly turn around and attack.'

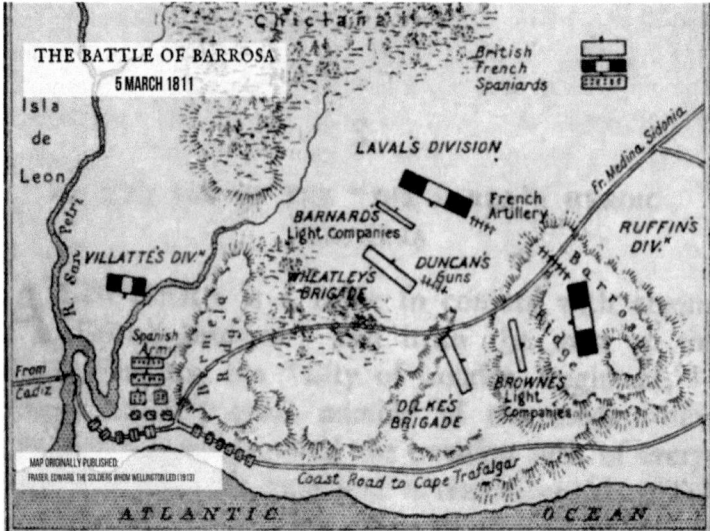

THE BATTLE OF BARROSA
5 MARCH 1811

British
French
Spaniards

Isla de Leon

LAVAL'S DIVISION

Fr. Medina Sidonia

BARNARD'S Light Companies

French Artillery

RUFFIN'S DIV.

VILLATTE'S DIV.

DUNCAN'S 4 Guns

WHEATLEY'S BRIGADE

Spanish Army

From Cadiz

DILKE'S BRIGADE

BROWNE'S Light Companies

MAP ORIGINALLY PUBLISHED:
FRASER, EDWARD, THE SOLDIERS WHOM WELLINGTON LED (1913)

Coast Road to Cape Trafalgar

ATLANTIC   OCEAN

Our old friend Robert Blakeney was alongside Lieutenant Colonel Browne and wrote:

> The flank battalion were instantly extended into skirmishing order, which had scarcely been done when the general again rode back to Colonel Browne, saying, 'I must show something more serious than skirmishing; close the men into compact battalion.' 'That I will, with pleasure,' cried the colonel 'for it is more in my way than light bobbing.' The order to close on the centre was instantly bugled out, during which movement the colonel sent to know from the general, who had again retired, if he was to advance as soon as formed, and whether he was to attack immediately in his front or more towards his right. The answer was, 'attack in your front, and immediately.' All being now ready. Colonel Browne rode to the front of the battalion and taking off his hat said in a voice to be heard by all, 'Gentlemen, I am happy to be the bearer of good news: General Graham has done you the honour of being the first to attack those fellows. Now follow me you rascals.' He pointed to the enemy, and giving the order to advance broke into his favourite air: 'Now, cheer up, my brave lads! To glory we steer, to add something new to this wonderful year.' Thus, we moved forward with four hundred and sixty-eight men and twenty-one officers to attack the position, upon which but three-quarters of an hour previously we had

stood in proud defiance of the advancing foe, but which was now defended by two thousand five hundred infantry and eight pieces of artillery, together with some cavalry.[69]

As Browne's attack to retake the heights began, the green-clad British riflemen at the other end of the line, about a mile further north, also began to skirmish forward to interrupt and delay General Leval's division, which was closing fast. Sergeant William Surtees, who, because of his position as Quartermaster, had the distinction of riding a horse, recalled:

Those immediately in front of my battalion were the famed 8th regiment and consisted of two battalions of 700 men each; one was composed of grenadiers, and the other of voltigeurs, or light infantry. The grenadiers had long waving red plumes in their caps, at least a foot in length; while the light infantry had feathers of the same length and make, but green, with yellow tops. The whole of the French army had on their best or holyday suits of clothing, with their arms as bright as silver, and glancing in the sun as they moved in column, gave them really a noble and martial appearance. We had no sooner cleared the wood than we inclined to our left and went immediately at them. Major Duncan's guns commenced playing upon their column the moment he could get a clear piece of ground. The two companies of the 47th, attached to my battalion, were taken to cover and remain with the guns. Our people extended as we went up the hill, the Portuguese supporting us in the rear; and in a very short time we were hotly engaged with the fellows with the beautiful green feathers, many of which fell on the ground in a short time. As we advanced, the battalions to our right and in rear of us got formed in line, and moving forward in fine style, took up stronger ground in advance; the guns in the centre also moving onward, and causing dreadful havoc in the enemy's ranks. Early in the action my horse was killed, being shot in the head, which ball, had his head not stopped it, would in all probability have entered my body. He fell like a stone. I then went on and joined the ranks and finding a rifle of a man that had just fallen, (poor little Croudace's servant, who afterwards fell himself,) I took a few shots at them in revenge for my horse.[70]

Browne's Flank Battalion on the right, and the men of the 95th on the left, outnumbered and outgunned, were buying precious time for Graham to reorganise and reform his main body. But it was deadly work as Blakeney testified:

> As soon as we crossed the ravine close to the base of the hill and formed on the opposite side, a most tremendous roar of cannon and musketry was all at once opened, Rufin's whole division pointing at us with muskets, and eight pieces of ordnance sending forth their grape, firing as one salvo. Nearly two hundred of our men and more than half the officers went down by this first volley, thus opening the battle propitiously for them. We now literally stood in extended order; the battalion was checked. In closing on the centre and endeavouring to form a second efficient line, upwards of fifty more men and some officers were levelled with the earth; and all the exertions of Colonel Browne could not form a third line. We had by this time lost upwards of two hundred and fifty men and fourteen officers, between killed and wounded; the remainder of the battalion now scattered. The men commenced firing from behind trees, mounds or any cover which presented, and could not be got together. [71]

Seeing the bloodshed and confusion amongst Browne's men, Brigadier General William Thomas Dilkes now steered his brigade of guardsmen further to the right, where there was more cover. His men lost their formation in the woods but continued to press forward, emerging from the tree line on the right of the Flank Battalion. Marshal Victor, seeing his opportunity, threw four battalions at the Guards. The French advanced in column downhill with every expectation of a quick and glorious victory. But Victor had underestimated the fighting prowess of the Guards. The historian Sir Charles Oman brilliantly described what happened next:

> This was the crisis of the battle in the southern half of its progress. By all the rules of French military art four battalion columns, fresh and well ordered, charging downhill, should have been able to break through a disordered line of decidedly inferior strength pushing upwards against them. Dilkes had only 1,400 men, the four French battalions just over 2,000. Nevertheless, the impossible happened. When the two columns of the 24th Ligne came down, with drums beating and levelled bayonets,

against the centre of the firm, if disorderly, line in front, they were checked by the furious fire that broke out against them from the semicircle into which they had pushed. This was one more example of the fact established at Maida five years before, and reaffirmed at Vimeiro, Talavera, and Bussaco, that no column could break the British line by mere impetus.[72]

'B'JABERS BOYS, OI'VE GOT THE CUCKOO'

Further north, on the British left flank, Colonel William Wheatley's brigade was emerging from the woods to tackle General Jean Francois Leval's Division. Amongst them were the Irishmen of the 2/87th Regiment of Foot commanded by Major Hugh Gough. They rushed forward with a rousing cry of *'Faugh-a-Ballagh'* (Gaelic for 'clear the way'). The redcoats smashed into the Frenchmen of the 8th *Ligne,* who were still in column formation and could not get away. It was a brutal fight, the Irishmen in a furious rage and keen for blood. Ensign Edward Keogh, at the forefront of the attack, looked through the drifting smoke and spotted the top of a French Eagle standard, its gold plating glinting in the sun. The Eagles, like British colours, were the heart and soul of a French regiment – to capture one would bring a man and his unit immortal glory. Keogh called to Sergeant Patrick Masterson and together they waded into the fray, the young Ensign swinging his sword with deadly precision. Edward Fraser, in his book *The soldiers whom Wellington led*, describes what happened next:

> At once he closed with the Frenchman, and crossed swords, with his left hand making a grab at the Eagle pole. Keogh got hold of it and tried to pull it away, but he could not wrench it free before the brave Ensign went down with half a dozen musket-bullets and two bayonet-stabs in his body. According to French accounts, *Porte-Aigle* [Ensign] Guillemin, as the Eagle-bearer of the 8th was named, fell dead at the same moment as Ensign Keogh, shot through the head by one of the British privates. Other Frenchmen rushed up then to rescue the Eagle, and formed round it hastily. One of the British privates who had seized hold of the staff as Keogh fell was slashed to death, and once more the French recovered it. But they were not to keep it unchallenged. A close

and desperately furious tussle followed. Seven French officers and sub-officers the records of the regiment state fell dead in gallantly defending the Eagle. An eighth, Lieutenant Gazan, clung to the pole desperately with both hands, regardless of wounds that nearly hacked him to pieces. Finally, the Eagle was torn from his grasp by Sergeant Masterson, who remained at the end the sole unwounded survivor of the attacking British party. Gazan 'survived miraculously,' we are told, and lived to be decorated by Napoleon for his devoted courage. Sergeant Masterson carried the Eagle off and kept it.[73]

As Sergeant Masterson waved his trophy in the air, it is claimed he shouted, *'B'jabers boys, Oi've got the cuckoo.'* It was the first Imperial Eagle the British had captured during the Peninsular War and the triumphant Sergeant was rewarded for his valour with a commission to the rank of Ensign. He remained in the army, eventually becoming a captain and retiring in 1828.[74]

General Leval, realising that the battle was in danger of being lost, threw the 54th Regiment forward against the British left flank. These fresh troops hesitated in the face of the furious redcoats and fell back under pressure from the men of the 28th Regiment of Foot who battered them with rolling volleys and then charged with the bayonet. Charles Cadell, an officer of the 28th, later wrote:

> We formed line under cover of the 95th (Rifles), and advanced to meet their right wing, which was then coming down in close column; this gave us a great advantage, and here the coolness of Colonel Belson was conspicuous; we being the left regiment, he moved us up without firing a shot, close to their right battalion, which just began to deploy. Colonel Belson then gave orders to fire by platoons from centre to flanks, at the same time, 'to be sure to fire at their legs and spoil their dancing;' – this order was observed for a short time with dreadful effect. The action now become general; twice did we attempt to charge the enemy, who being double our strength (our flank companies being away) only retired a little. Giving three cheers, we charged a third time, and succeeded, the enemy gave way, and fled in every direction; in less than two hours they had been beaten in every part of the field. God was pleased to grant to the British arms as glorious and complete victory as ever was gained.[75]

Cadell was not wrong, Leval's entire division now fell back, joining with the battered remnants of the other French units as they retreated in haste back to their camp at Chiclana. Against tremendous odds, the battle was won, and the French were beaten. Lieutenant General Graham had found himself surprised by an experienced and capable enemy commander, he had lost the key feature at the start of the battle and yet, thanks to the bravery and elan of his redcoats and riflemen, a dire situation had been retrieved and a noteworthy victory was achieved.

Graham in his despatch to Wellington wrote:

> No expressions of mine could do justice to the conduct of the troops throughout. Nothing less than the almost unparalleled exertions of every officer, the invincible bravery of every soldier, and the most determined devotion to the honour of His Majesty's arms in all, could have achieved this brilliant success against such a formidable enemy so posted. In less than an hour and a half from the commencement of the action the enemy was in full retreat. . . the exhausted state of the troops made pursuit impossible.[76]

THE AFTERMATH

British casualties during the battle were 1,238. Some units had been hit particularly hard. The companies of the 28th Regiment of Foot that were attached to Lieutenant Colonel Browne's Flank Battalion lost a staggering two-thirds of their men and all of their officers killed or wounded.

The French had suffered a little over 2,000 men killed, wounded, and captured – almost one third of Victor's force. They also had the indignity of losing six pieces of artillery and an Imperial Eagle – a very heavy toll for such a brief battle. Sergeant William Surtees witnessed the sad reality behind these casualty numbers:

> My battalion was still standing in front of the position last occupied by our troops, all having retired but ourselves, and it now began to draw towards night, and we were preparing to

move off, an unfortunate French sergeant attracted our notice. Poor fellow, he had been shot in the small of the back, and (on our surgeon examining him) pronounced to be mortally. He appeared to be a man above forty, and apparently a veteran, who had fought many a hard field; and was, I think, one of the most respectable-looking men of his class that I have seen. When he saw us preparing to leave him to his fate, the expression of his countenance became the most piteous and beseeching imaginable; imploring us in French not to leave him there to perish. My heart bled for him; but unhappily we had no means of removing him, had there even been a hope of his recovery. When he saw that his fate was inevitable, he crawled in the best manner he was able to a broken ammunition-box, and raising himself on his knees, supported by it, besought that Being who never casts out the cry of the unfortunate, and who, I sincerely hope, imparted to him that strength and comfort which his unhappy circumstances so greatly required. I doubt not he was a sincere Christian; never shall I forget the impression his unhappy fate made on my mind. To be left in solitude and darkness on this blood-stained heath, with the prospect of his own certain death before his eyes, and without any to comfort him in his last agony, must indeed have been a severe trial to his fortitude. Would to God I could have relieved him! His case was not singular, it is true; but none ever presented itself to my view under such truly affecting circumstances as this unhappy veteran's did.[77]

Despite the glory that was hard-earned by the British soldiers, there was no strategic triumph. General La Peña had refused to march his men to the sound of the guns and so only a tiny number of his 10,000 men had joined the fight – behaviour that Oman calls *'astounding'* and *'selfish.'* If he had shown boldness, then there was every chance that Victor's army could have been crushed and the siege raised. Lieutenant General Graham, livid at the lack of support he had received, had no wish to conduct any further operations alongside the Spanish and marched his men back into Cadiz. The Allies were now back where they had begun two weeks before.

CHAPTER FIVE: FOUNTAIN OF HONOUR – THE BATTLE OF FUENTES DE OÑORO

WELLINGTON SPLITS HIS ARMY

As the Battle of Barossa was being fought outside Cadiz, the situation was also developing rapidly for Wellington and the troops in Portugal.

During the Allied pursuit of Masséna, developments along the southern border forced Wellington to split his army. French Marshal Jean de Dieu Soult had advanced from Seville and began siege operations against the vitally important border-city of Badajoz. If the city fell, then Soult could potentially advance into Portugal by the southern route. But, with its broad ditch, high walls and its ring of outlying forts, Badajoz was an exceptionally strong bastion on the banks of the Guadiana River. It had a garrison of nearly 5,000 Spanish troops – seemingly more than enough for a successful defence.

At the beginning of March 1811, Marshal William Carr Beresford was given command of around 18,000 men, including the 2nd and 4th Divisions, and ordered to relieve Badajoz. But, shortly after his force of British and Portuguese troops began their advance, the strategic situation changed once again. The Spanish commander at Badajoz, General José Imaz, despite his formidable position, strong artillery compliment, plentiful food supplies and the knowledge that a relief force was on its way, inexplicably surrendered on the 10th of March. This meant that Beresford's relief force was now tasked with mounting its own siege of Badajoz – a role for which it was ill-prepared.

While this drama played out, the rest of Wellington's troops were kept in the north to shadow Masséna's battered army. Wellington, understandably, assumed that Masséna would need a considerable amount of time to re-equip and reorganise his troops after their ordeal in Portugal. But he underestimated the Marshal's abilities and his capacity to recover. In fact, Masséna, keen to impress

Napoleon, had soon gathered close to 50,000 men and started marching back towards Portugal. His objective was to relieve and resupply the French garrison that was besieged and holding out in the border fortress of Almeida.

It was imperative that the French were stopped from reaching Almeida. Wellington needed control of all the key border fortresses if he was to resume the offensive and advance into Spain.

When news of Massena's advance reached the British, Wellington was outside Badajoz giving instructions to Beresford for his upcoming siege. Wellington rushed north and, to the great relief of the British soldiers, he arrived back on the 29th of April 1811. John Kincaid of the 95th wrote:

> As a general action seemed now to be inevitable, we anxiously longed for the return of Lord Wellington. . .as we would rather see his long nose in the fight than a reinforcement of 10,000 men any day. Indeed, there was a charm not only about himself, but all connected with him, for which no odds could compensate.[78]

Wellington immediately concentrated his divisions for battle. But the ground wasn't favourable – there were no steep ridge lines or rolling hills to defend. Therefore, he was forced to make the best of the terrain – and that was a position by the village of Fuentes de Oñoro. The small Spanish village sits astride the road along which the enemy was advancing between Ciudad Rodrigo and Almeida. It was (and still is) a jumble of narrow alleys, small cottages, and high stone walls. On the edge of the village running north to south is the narrow and easily fordable Dos Casas River.

The village, with its excellent cover and concealment, was the linchpin of Wellington's defence. But his Achilles heel was the ground beyond his right flank – in particular, towards the village of Poço Velho (often referred to as Pozzo Bello), three miles further south. Here, the terrain was good for cavalry and could potentially allow the French to outflank the Allied force. If the right flank was turned, then the British and Portuguese army would be cut off from their easiest line of retreat to Portugal. Another major cause for concern for the British was the proximity of the Coa River which ran just six miles behind the line. Should the impending battle go in favour of the French, the retreating Allied forces could be caught and slaughtered while trying to cross to safety.

Wellington had at his disposal 34,000 infantry, of which 23,000 were British, nearly 2,000 cavalry and 48 guns.[79] He felt confident that this force was sufficient. The 5th and 6th Divisions were tasked with holding his naturally strong left flank, which was anchored by the derelict but still formidable, Fort Concepcion. The 1st, 3rd, the newly formed 7th Division, and the Light Division were deployed around Fuentes De Oñoro. Inside the village, 28 detached companies of light troops and riflemen (over 2,000 men in total) were posted under the command of Lieutenant-Colonel William Williams of the 5/60th Rifles. Light troops, experienced in skirmishing and working in small detachments were well suited to the challenges of fighting in built-up areas where command and control would soon be lost in the confusion of a street fight.

THE BATTLE OF FUENTES DE OÑORO BEGINS, 3 MAY 1811

On the 3rd of May, Masséna's army pushed back the Allied outposts and approached Wellington's position. Joseph Donaldson of the 94th wrote:

> The morning was uncommonly beautiful. The sun shone bright and warm, the various odiferous shrubs, which were scattered profusely around, perfumed the air, and the woods rang with the songs of birds. The Light Division and the cavalry falling back, followed by the columns of the French, the various divisions of the army assembling on the plane from different quarters, their arms glittering in the sun, bugles blowing, drums beating, the various staff-officers galloping about to different parts of the line giving orders, formed a scene which realized to my mind all that I had ever read of feats of arms or the pomp of war; a scene which no one could behold unmoved, or without feeling a portion of that enthusiasm which always accompanies 'deeds of high daring'.[80]

The French columns were now clearly visible to the British generals. The French 2nd Corps, under the command of General Jean Reynier, deployed opposite Fort Concepcion. On their left was a single division of the 8th Corps. Then came the thick mass of five entire divisions from the 6th and 9th Corps, which formed up opposite the village. Masséna, like Wellington, clearly recognised that the village of Fuentes de Oñoro as the key to the battle.

In the early afternoon, Masséna ordered the first attack against the village. As the French skirmishers and cavalry moved forward, Donaldson witnessed a bizarre and amusing incident:

The [French] skirmishers were covered in their advance by cavalry, in consequence of which ours were obliged to fall back. . .while a party of our German hussars covered their retreat. The cavalry now commenced skirmishing, the infantry keeping up an occasional fire. It was rather remarkable that the cavalry on both sides happened to be Germans. When this was understood volleys of insulting language were exchanged between them. One of our hussars got so enraged at something one of his opponents said that he dashed forward upon him into the very centre of their line. The French hussar, seeing that he had no mercy to expect from his enraged foe, wheeled about his horse, and rode to the rear; the other, determined on revenge, still continued to follow him. The whole attention of both sides was drawn for a moment, to these two, and a temporary cessation of firing took place; the French staring in astonishment at our hussar's temerity, while our men were cheering him on. The chase continued for some way to the rear of their cavalry. At last our hussar coming up with him, and fetching a furious blow, brought him to the ground. Awakening now to the sense of danger he had thrown himself into, he set his horse at full speed to get back to his comrades; but the French who were confounded when he passed, had recovered from their surprise, and determined on revenging the death of their comrade; they joined in the pursuit firing their pistols at him. The poor fellow was now in a hazardous plight; they were every moment gaining on him, and he still had a long way to ride. A band of the enemy took a circuit for the purpose of intercepting him; and before he could reach the lines he was surrounded, and would have been cut to pieces, had not a party of his comrades, stimulated by the wish to save so brave a fellow, rushed forward, and just arrived in time, by making the attack general, to save his life, and brought him off in triumph.[81]

Three thick French columns advanced behind their skirmishers and pushed the Allied light troops back through the village.

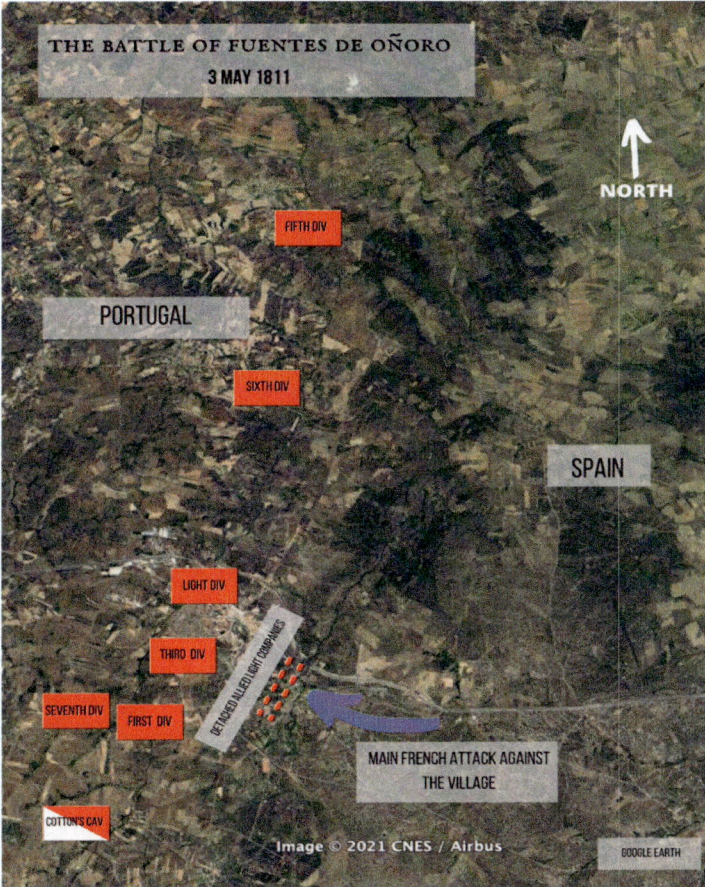

It was a brutal close-range engagement – a street fight at the point of the bayonet. In the narrow alleys, it was hard to keep formation and for officers to maintain control; the fight became brutal and personal. Slowly, the first brigade of General Claude Ferey's division gained a foothold in the houses on the lower slope.

At this moment the French might have completely routed the British if plunder had not distracted them. Donaldson remembered:

> The overwhelming force which the French now pushed forward on the village, could not be withstood by the small number of troops which defended it; they were obliged to give way, and were fairly forced to a rising ground on the other side, where stood a small chapel. . .While retreating through the town one of our sergeants who had run up the wrong street, being pushed hard by the enemy ran into one of the houses: They were close at his heels; and he had just time to tumble himself into a large chest, and let the lid down, when they entered and commenced plundering the house, expressing their wonder at the same time as to the sudden disappearance of the '*Anglois*' whom they had seen run into the house. During this time the poor sergeant lay sweating and half smothered; they were busy breaking up everything that came in their way, looking for plunder; and they were in the act opening the lid of his hiding place, when the noise of our men cheering, as they charged through the town, forced them to take flight.[82]

A well-timed counter-attack had saved the lucky sergeant. Lieutenant Colonel Williams used his small reserve to drive the French back out of the village. But there was no time for the defenders to rest. General Ferey immediately threw his Second Brigade forward and once again, the British were forced back. These fresh French soldiers surged through the maze of houses and alleyways, nearly capturing the entire village.

Wellington, watching closely from the slopes behind Fuentes de Oñoro, saw his opportunity and, at around 3p.m., ordered a counter-attack by the 71st, 79th and 2/24th regiments. Thomas Pococke, of the 71st (Highland) Regiment of Foot, recalled what happened next:

> Colonel Cadogan put himself at our head, saying 'My lads, you have had no provision these two days; there is plenty in the hollow in front, let us down and divide it.' We advanced, as quick as we could run, and met the light companies retreating as fast as they could. We continued to advance, at double-quick time, our firelocks at the trail, our bonnets in our hands. They called to

us, 'Seventy-first, you will come back quicker than you advance.' We soon came full in front of the enemy. The Colonel cried, 'Here is food, my lads, cut away.' Thrice we waved our bonnets, and thrice we cheered; brought our firelocks to the charge, and forced them back through the town. . .the British officers, restraining their men, still as death — 'Steady, lads, steady,' is all; you hear; and that in an under tone. The French had lost a great number of men in the streets. We pursued them about a mile out of the town, trampling over the dead and wounded; but their cavalry bore down upon us and forced us back into the town, where we kept our ground in spite of their utmost efforts. In this affair my life was most wonderfully preserved. In forcing the French through the towns, during our first advance, a bayonet went through between my side and clothes to my knapsack, which stopped its progress. The Frenchman to whom the bayonet belonged, fell, pierced by a musket ball from my rear-rank man. Whilst freeing myself from the bayonet, a ball took off part of my right shoulder wing, and killed my rear rank man, who fell upon me. Narrow as this escape was, I felt no uneasiness, I had become so inured to danger and fatigue.[83]

The British counter-attack had been bloody, but successful. But Masséna wasn't finished for the day. He was still intent on capturing the village and ordered the battered survivors of Ferey's division to attack once more – this time supported by four additional battalions from General Jean Gabriel Marchand's division.

Despite the large number of men, the French advance faltered under the heavy fire of the redcoats. With the coming of darkness, the day's fighting finally petered out. The French had suffered nearly 700 casualties trying to take the village, while the Allied defenders had lost 259 – including their commander Lieutenant Colonel Williams who was badly wounded. During the day's fighting, Thomas Pococke, said that his shoulder was 'black as coal' after firing 107 musket balls – an impressive number, and testament to the fierceness of the fight.

The next morning, despite some light skirmishing, there was an informal truce, Pococke recalled:

I was awakened by the loud call of the bugle, an hour before day.

Soon as it was light the firing commenced, and was kept up until about ten o'clock, when Lieutenant Stewart, of our regiment, was sent with a flag of truce, for leave to carry off our wounded from the enemy's lines, which was granted, and at the same time they carried off theirs from ours. As soon as the wounded were all got in, many of whom had lain bleeding all night. . .the French brought down a number of bands of music to a level piece of ground, about ninety or a hundred yards broad, that lay between us. They continued to play until sunset, whilst the men were dancing and diverting themselves at football. We were busy cooking the remainder of our sausages, bacon, and flour.[84]

THE FIGHT FOR THE RIGHT FLANK, 5TH OF MAY 1811

In the French camp, Masséna was deep in thought and reworking his plan of attack. Once again, as at Busacco, he had been taught how stubborn the British and Portuguese were in defence. As the opposing armies collected their wounded and listened to their bands play on the 4th of May, he sent cavalry General Louis-Pierre Montbrun to recce the British right flank and to discover if it could be turned. The result of his mission was promising – the villages of Nave de Haver and Poço Velho, just under 4 km south of Fuentes de Oñoro, were lightly held by the Allies and offered an opportunity for the French cavalry to be let loose.

Upon hearing Montbrun's report, Masséna refocused his attack and, after dusk, he began deploying three infantry divisions and nearly all of his cavalry – a total of 17,000 infantry and 3,500 sabres – to take advantage of the Allied weakness. The new plan was to hit the Allied right flank hard at first light on the 5th of May and then, as Wellington inevitably rushed reserves to stop them, Masséna would once again renew his brutal frontal attack against the village of Fuentes de Oñoro.

Wellington realised that the pause in the fighting on the 4th was most likely a prelude to a French attempt to roll up his lightly defended right. He therefore moved the 7th Division – the weakest and least experienced in his army – to stiffen that flank. With hindsight, that seems a poor decision by Wellington. It left the 7th Division incredibly exposed, a long way from support. Wellington was in a difficult spot here, he needed to protect his right flank and keep open the road that led south back into central Portugal, but he was also determined to stop the French attempt to relieve Almeida – he didn't have enough men to do both.

The 7th Division under Major-General John Houston took up their new position. Two battalions were posted inside the village of Poço Velho – the 85th Regiment of Foot and the Portuguese 2nd Caçadores. The rest of the division was deployed on the open slopes slightly to the west. It was poor ground for a prolonged defence. Houston and his men had been given an incredibly tough task – perhaps one better suited to a more experienced division.

As the sun rose, chasing away the early morning chill on the 5th of May, the French began their assault. First into action was the cavalry. William Tomkinson of the 16th Light Dragoons, recalled the start of the fight:

> Our two brigades of cavalry scarcely amounted to 900, and these in bad condition. The enemy had 4,000 fresh cavalry and were driving ours back on the infantry. . .Major Myers of the Hussars was in advance with two squadrons — one from the 16th, and one of his own regiment. Captain Belli had joined from England the day before, and taken the command of Captain Cocks' squadron. Cocks commanded the left. Captain Belli's squadron, with one of the Hussars, was in advance; and the enemy having sent forward two or three squadrons. Major Myers attempted to oppose them in front of a defile. He waited so long and was so indecisive, and the enemy came up so close, that he ordered the squadron of the 16th to charge. The enemy's squadron was about twice their strength, and waited their charge. This is the only instance I ever met with of two bodies of cavalry coming in opposition, and both standing, as invariably, as I have observed it, one or the other runs away. Our men rode up and began sabering, but were so outnumbered that they could do nothing, and were obliged to retire across the defile in confusion, the enemy having brought up more troops to that point. Captain Belli was wounded slightly, and taken; Sergeant Taylor, of his own troop, and six men from the squadron, were killed on the spot in attempting to rescue

him. The enemy cannonaded the cavalry a good deal in retiring, in which we lost Lieutenant Blake of the 16th. He was hit by a four-pound shot in the thigh, and, through some mistake, the shot was not taken out, and he rode with it to Castel Mendo, where a Portuguese surgeon took it out.[85]

Shortly afterwards, the beating of drums and the heavy fire of skirmishers showed the advance of the French infantry into the village of Poço Velho. They soon forced the heavily outnumbered men of the 85th Regiment and 2nd Caçadores to withdraw. This was an incredibly dangerous moment – far from support. In the open and at the mercy of enemy cavalry, the two Allied battalions had a mammoth task ahead of them. The French cavalry, sensing blood, pounced on the disordered troops and began inflicting heavy casualties on them. The survivors were rescued from annihilation by the timely intervention of two squadrons of Wellington's German Hussars.

Standing nearby, amongst the ranks of the 7th Division, was Private William Wheeler of the 2/51st Regiment:

Our position after throwing back our right wing was about 20 paces under the brow of a gentle descent beyond which was a large plane covered with the enemy. A little distance in our rear the ground began to rise rather abruptly, it was covered with cork trees, rocks and straggling bushes, there was also a long wall behind us. On the high ground this was occupied by the Chasseurs Britanniques Regiment [a unit composed mainly of French deserters] and the Portuguese Brigade. We had some men in our front skirmishing, but they were soon driven in and formed with us, thus situated we anxiously awaited the attack. An officer of Huzzars [sic] soon showed himself on the brow, he viewed us with much attention then coolly turned around in his saddle and waved his sword. In an instant the brow was covered with cavalry. This was a critical moment; the least unsteadiness would have caused confusion. This would have been followed with defeat and disgrace. The enemy had walked to the brow, and their trumpeter was sounding the charge, when Colonel Mainwaring gave the words, 'Ready, Present, Fire.' For a moment the smoke hindered us from seeing the effect of our fire, but we soon saw plenty of horses stretched not many yards from us. The Chasseurs Britanniques Regiment now opened a fire, as did the

Portuguese, over our heads. It was a dangerous but necessary expedient, for our fire was not sufficient to stop the cavalry, so we were obliged to lay down and load.[86]

Wellington, realising the extent and scale of the French assault against his right, called upon the trusty Light Division to advance south and assist the 7th to safety. With General Craufurd back from leave, replacing the incompetent General William Erskine, the men were in high spirits as they marched to the sound of the guns. Captain John Kincaid was with them:

> Our battalion was thrown into a wood, a little to the left and front of the division engaged, and was instantly warmly opposed by the French skirmishers; in the course of which I was struck with a musket-ball on the left breast, which made me stagger a yard or two backward, and, as I felt no pain, I concluded that I was dangerously wounded; but it turned out to be owing to my not being hurt. While our operations here were confined to a tame skirmish, and our view to the oaks with which we were mingled, we found, by the evidence of our ears, that the division which we had come to support was involved in a more serious onset, for there was the successive rattle of artillery, the wild hurrah of charging squadrons, and the repulsing volley of musketry.[87]

It was certainly a serious situation for the 7th Division. Private Wheeler continues:

> The enemy had formed again and was ready for another attack, our force was not sufficient to repel such a mass, so the order was given to retire independently by regiments. We retired through the broken ground in our rear, crossed the wall, and was pretty safe from their cavalry, but they had brought up their guns to the brow and was serving out the shot with a liberal hand. We continued retiring and soon came to a narrow rapid stream, this we waded up to our armpits and from the steepness of the opposite bank we found much difficulty in getting out. This caused some delay so the Regiment waited until all had crossed, then formed line and continued our retreat in quick time. . .Thanks to Colonel Mainwaring we came off safe, although the shot was flying pretty thick, yet his superior skill baffled all the efforts of the enemy, he took advantage of the ground and led us

out of the scrape without loss.[88]

General Craufurd and the Light Division had now arrived, the battalions 'going firm', allowing the 7th to fall back in good order. The Light Division, supported by a General Stapleton Cotton's cavalry, was immediately assailed by over 3,000 French horsemen, the best part of three infantry divisions and several batteries of artillery. The great Peninsular war historian William Napier says of this moment, 'There was not, during the war, a more dangerous hour for England'[89]

Craufurd, understanding that he could not allow the men to be pinned down by artillery, or be caught in the open by the cavalry, formed his battalions into receive cavalry squares as they slowly retired to the north. The division maintained perfect order as they withdrew, the bristling wall of bayonets keeping the French cavalry at bay. This expert manoeuvring, in the face of the enemy, was testament to their training and experience. The historian Jac Weller describes this as 'Craufurd's finest hour.'

Meanwhile, Captain Robert Bull's troop of Horse Artillery prowled the battlefield offering much-needed fire support. There was one heart stopping moment when Captain Norman Ramsey's two guns were surrounded by French cavalry. It seemed that all was lost. . .but his men coolly limbered their guns and drew their swords – slashing and cutting their way through the mass of Frenchmen to safety, emerging through the smoke to the cheers of their comrades. It is a moment captured in several well-known paintings of the battle.

Despite suffering some casualties to the French artillery, the Light Division reached the safety of the new British line, which faced south at a right angle to Fuentes de Oñoro.

THE FINAL BATTLE FOR THE VILLAGE

Marshal Masséna now switched his focus back to the village. He wanted a stand-up brawl, to smash through the British line with three entire infantry divisions. Thomas Pococke was one of the redcoats waiting for them:

72

Down they came, shouting as usual. We kept them at bay, in spite of their cries and formidable looks. How different their appearance from ours! Their hats set round with feathers, their beards long and black, gave them a fierce look. Their stature was superior to ours; most of us were young. We looked like boys; they like savages. But we had the true spirit in us. We foiled them in every attempt to take the town, until about eleven o'clock, when we were overpowered, and forced through the streets, contesting every inch. A French dragoon, who was dealing death around, forced his way up to near where I stood. Every moment I expected to be cut down. My piece was empty; there was not a moment to lose. I got a stab at him, beneath the ribs, upwards; he gave a back stroke, before he fell, and cut the stock of my musket in two; thus, I stood unarmed. I soon got another, and fell to work again.[90]

Just behind the village were the hard-fighting Irishmen of the 88th (part of Major General Thomas Picton's 3rd Division), amongst them was Captain William Grattan, who recalled:

Every street, and every angle of a street, were the different theatres for the combatants; inch by inch was gained and lost in turn. Whenever the enemy were forced back, fresh troops, and fresh energy on the part of their officers, impelled them on again, and towards mid-day the town presented a shocking sight; our Highlanders lay dead in heaps, while the other regiments, though less remarkable in dress, were scarcely so in the numbers of their slain. The French Grenadiers, with their immense caps and gaudy plumes, in piles of twenty and thirty together—some dead, others wounded, with barely strength sufficient to move; their exhausted state, and the weight of their cumbrous appointments, making it impossible for them to crawl out of the range of the dreadful fire of grape and round shot which the enemy poured into the town. Great numbers perished in this way, and many were pressed to death in the streets.[91]

But the French, in their desperation, kept coming and eventually through the weight of their numbers pushed the redcoats out of the village and onto the slopes beyond. At this point Grattan, stood on the high ground overlooking the village, witnessed an important conversation between his regiment's commanding officer,

Colonel Wallace, and Sir Edward Packenham (Wellington's brother-in-law) that lead to the decisive counterattack:

Sir Edward Pakenham galloped up to him [Wallace], and said, 'Do you see that, Wallace?' 'I do,' replied the Colonel, 'and I would rather drive the French out of the town than cover a retreat across the Coa.' 'Perhaps,' said Sir Edward, 'his lordship don't think it tenable.' Wallace answering said, 'I shall take it with my regiment, and keep it too.' — 'Will you?' was the reply; 'I'll go and tell Lord Wellington so; see, here he comes.' In a moment or two Pakenham returned at a gallop, and, waving his hat, called out, 'He says you may go come along, Wallace.'[92]

Grattan continues:

The battalion advanced with fixed bayonets in column of sections, left in front, in double quick time, their firelocks at the trail. As it passed down the road leading to the chapel, it was warmly cheered by the troops that lay at each side of the wall, but the soldiers made no reply to this greeting. They were placed in a situation of great distinction, and they felt it; they were going to fight, not only under the eye of their own army and general, but also in the view of every soldier in the French army; but although their feelings were wrought up to the highest pitch of enthusiasm, not one hurrah responded to the shouts that welcomed their advance. There was no noise or talking in the ranks; the men stepped together at a smart trot, as if on a parade, headed by their brave colonel. It so happened that the command of the company which led this attack devolved upon me. When we came within sight of the French 9th Regiment, which were drawn up at the corner of the chapel, waiting for us, I turned around to look at the men of my company; they gave me a cheer that a lapse of many years has not made me forget, and I thought that that moment was the proudest of my life. The soldiers did not look as men usually do going into close fight — pale, the trot down the road had heightened their complexions, and they were the picture of everything that a chosen body of troops ought to be. The enemy were not idle spectators of this movement they witnessed its commencement, and the regularity with which the advance was conducted made them fearful of the result. A battery of eight-pounders advanced at a gallop to an olive-grove on the opposite bank of the river, hoping by the effects of its fire to annihilate the 88th Regiment, or, at all events, embarrass its movements as much as possible but this battalion continued to press on, joined by its exhausted comrades, and the battery did little execution. On reaching the head of the village, the 88th Regiment was vigorously opposed by the French 9th Regiment, supported by some hundred [men] of the Imperial Guard[93], but it soon closed in with them, and, aided by the brave fellows that had so gallantly fought in the town all the morning, drove the enemy through the different streets at the point of the bayonet, and at length forced them into the river that separated the two armies. Several of our men fell on the French side of the water. About one hundred and fifty of the grenadiers of the Guard, in their flight, ran down a street that had been barricaded by us the day before, and which was one of the few that escaped the fury of the morning's assault; but their disappointment was great, upon arriving at the bottom, to find themselves shut in. Mistakes of this kind will sometimes occur, and when they do, the result is easily imagined; troops advancing to assault a town, uncertain of success, or flushed with victory, have no great time to deliberate as to what they will do; the thing is generally done in half the time the deliberation would occupy. In the present instance, every man was put to death.[94]

The battle for the village had been a brutal gutter-fight. But the British had been victorious. By 2 p.m. the fighting had fizzled out. Without control of the village, and with his artillery outnumbered and out-gunned, Masséna realised that a general attack along the rest of the line was hopeless. But he didn't immediately withdraw, and so for the British, it wasn't clear if the battle was over. That night, expecting another French attack in the morning, Wellington ordered his troops to dig-in.

Subaltern George Simmons of the 95th Rifles recorded in his diary:

I was on picquet in the lower part of the village, near a little stream of water which passed through part of the town. The enemy had a captain's picquet on the opposite side of the little rill [a small stream], and a heavy column of infantry was formed behind a small church either waiting for orders or fearing an attack. We gave some badly wounded Frenchman to the picket, and the officer allowed some of ours to be given up. A French officer said to me, 'this place is appropriately named the Fountain of Honour; God knows how many of our friends on both sides have drunk deep of its waters, and with tomorrow's dawn most likely many more will do so.' My only reply to this was, 'the fortune of war will decide that, and we are ready to try its chances when our illustrious chief gives the order to advance.' The remainder of the night was occupied in knocking down many an honest man's garden wall and making a strong breastwork to fire over as soon as the day dawned.[95]

But when the sun rose, there was no renewal of the fighting. The battle had cost the British over 1,500 casualties, nearly a third of those amongst the 71st and 79th regiments[96] around the village of Fuentes de Oñoro. French casualties had been higher – over 2,000, with 1,300 of them sustained in the village.[97]

Marshal Masséna, incredibly frustrated by Wellington and the Allied troops, was forced, once again to withdraw. It was to be his last battle in the Peninsular. When he arrived in Ciudad Rodrigo two days later, his letter of dismissal was waiting for him. Napoleon's patience had expired. Despite Masséna's experience and his pedigree as commander, Wellington had bested him at every turn.

The Battle of Fuentes de Oñoro had been an incredibly close-run fight. The ground hadn't been particularly favourable for a prolonged defence, and the Allied right flank had come dangerously close to be being turned on the morning of the 5th of May. Wellington famously said afterwards, 'If *Boney* had been there, we should have been beaten.'[98]

Masséna's successor was Marshal Auguste Frédéric Louis Viesse de Marmont, a 36-year-old who had served alongside Napoleon at Toulon in 1793 and stuck by his side ever since. Marshal Marmont was almost the opposite of Masséna – educated and sophisticated, gentle, and caring with his men. But the question remained, could he achieve what his predecessors had not – victory over Wellington and his army?

CHAPTER SIX: THE BATTLE OF ALBUERA – BLOODIEST BATTLE OF THE WAR

On the 16th of May, just eleven days after the Battle of Fuentes de Oñoro, Marshal Beresford fought the bloodiest battle of the Peninsular War – the Battle of Albuera.

Beresford's force had been dispatched south by Wellington in March to relieve the Spanish at Badajoz, but the situation had drastically changed with the premature surrender of the garrison on the 10th – a turnaround that caught Wellington completely by surprise. He had been told by his allies that the fortress that covered the southern border between Spain and Portugal could hold out for at least another month.

Losing Badajoz was a major blow to Wellington. His plan for the rest of 1811 had been to consolidate his position around the northern Portuguese border – especially around the fort-cities of Almeida and Ciudad Rodrigo. But this plan was based on the premise that he had full control of the southern entry points at Badajoz and Elvas. Now, with a strong French force in control of Badajoz, his strategy was in tatters – the city needed to be retaken immediately.

THE FIRST SIEGE OF BADAJOZ

Beresford's 18,000[99] men were now tasked with conducting their own siege of the imposing border-city. Sieges are a serious business, and the Allied Peninsular army was very inexperienced in this form of warfare. As Major General John Jones wrote at the beginning of his three-volume history of the Peninsular War sieges:

> A siege is one of the most arduous undertakings on which troops can be employed, – an undertaking in which fatigue, hardships and personal risk are the greatest – one in which the prize can only be gained by complete victory, and where failure is usually with severe loss or dire disaster.[100]

The siege of Badajoz was a task for which Beresford's troops were not properly equipped. Lack of boats meant that their pontoon-bridge building efforts were delayed; thousands of men were without adequate footwear, food rations were running low and, most important of all, Beresford had a distinct lack of siege artillery. To remedy the situation, they requisitioned guns from the Portuguese fortress close by at Elvas – but these weapons were mainly antiques, some over 200 years old. Twenty-three guns and 400 half-trained artillerymen[101] were all that the British could muster for the siege. It was nowhere near enough.

Badajoz was a tough nut to crack. It was a large, fortified town on the left bank of the broad Guadiana River. Its walls were thirty-feet high and strong, with a large Moorish castle dominating the north-east angle of the defences. There were also four out-posts beyond the main wall: Fort Pardeleras; Fort Picurina; Fort San Cristoval; and San Roque, which was a small triangular outwork known as a *lunette*.

On the 22nd of April, Beresford and Wellington, who was making a flying visit from his northern headquarters, conducted a full reconnaissance of the city alongside their chief engineer – Lieutenant Colonel Sir Richard Fletcher. The next day, Wellington wrote three memoranda defining how he wished the siege to be conducted. Speed was of the essence – it was feared, with good reason, that should the capture of the city take longer than 16 days, then Marshal Soult would have time to concentrate his troops and march north from Seville to relieve Badajoz. Should this happen Beresford was given the freedom to decide how best to respond – whether to fight or to withdraw.

Another key aspect of Wellington's plan was the inclusion of local Spanish troops alongside his British and Portuguese. Previous operations with the Spanish had ended in frustration and disappointment, but Wellington was a pragmatist and understood that he needed their assistance once again. In a rare moment of solidarity, all the Spanish commanders operating in the region agreed to serve under Beresford should there be a general engagement. Given the pride of the Spanish and their general distrust of the British, this was a significant development. But would they be true to their word?

Captain Moyle Sherer of the 2/34th Regiment of Foot was part of Major General William Stewart's 2nd Division, and recalls the unit's final approach towards the imposing walls of Badajoz:

It was just at the dawn of the day, on the fourth, that the heads of all the columns destined to besiege Badajoz, crowned every little eminence round the city, and formed the investment of the place. Our previous night march had been well arranged as to time; and this operation, which is at all times interesting, was executed, on this occasion, with admirable skills and beautiful order. The sky was cloudless and serene, the morning air mild and pleasant. The enemy's picquets skirmished prettily with our advance, and they threw both and shots and shells from the town, but with little or no effect. They sent out the few dragoons they had, to assist in reconnoitring our force; and these men performed their duty with a degree of coolness and intrepidity which could not have been surpassed. I saw individuals ride up within pistol-shot of our infantry skirmishers; and one man galloped boldly as near to a column, not very distant from the height on which my regiment was formed. The scene was quite a review: The walls of Badajoz were crowded with spectators; and from the top of the castle the tri-coloured standard, an ensign which had spread terror over half of Europe, was calmly floating.[102]

The first step of the British plan was to capture Fort San Christoval before focusing on breaching the castle. But the approach to this commanding defensive work was more difficult than expected – the ground was hard and the British tools (pickaxes, etc) were of poor quality. The timetable set by Wellington quickly slipped.

For the Allied soldiers, most of whom were experiencing siege warfare for the first time, the work was laborious and backbreaking. Reading accounts, it is clear the experience was very similar to that their descendants would experience on the western front just over a hundred years later. Moyle Sherer wrote:

I regard the operations of a siege as highly interesting; the daily progress of the labours; the trenches filled with men, who lie secure within the range of the garrison; the fire of the batteries;

the beautiful appearance of the shells and fireballs by night; the challenge of the enemy's sentries; the sound of their drums and trumpets; all give a continued charm and animation to this service. But the duties of a besieging force are both harassing and severe; and I know. . .death in the trenches never carries with it that stamp of glory, which seals the memory of those who perish in a well-fought field.[103]

Our old friend, Sergeant John Spencer Cooper of the 2/7th Royal Fusiliers, recalled a story in his memoirs that illustrates the thin line between life and death in the siege trenches:

One day. . .while our company was in the trenches waiting for the engineer to stake out some more work, a party sat down to play cards in the trench. My duty was to warn the men of coming shot or shell. A burst of smoke: I bawled out— 'Take care.' Whew, whew, whew: all were silent. The shell strikes the ground, rebounds, rolls up the outside of the parapet, and falls over the shoulder of a card player, whose name was Arundel, into the trench between his legs. A scramble ensued. After a pause a soldier seized the shell and threw it out of the trench. When examined, 'twas found that by some means the fuse had been destroyed.[104]

On the 10th of May, the French launched an early morning sortie from Fort San Christoval. They took the British covering party by surprise and briefly occupied the position of the newly built gun battery. The defenders quickly rallied and counterattacked. Surgeon Charles Boutflower of the 40th Regiment takes up the story:

Unfortunately, our troops pursued them with their wonted ardour to the very walls, where they were exposed to a most destructive fire of shell shot and musquetry; notwithstanding with a very inferior force they completely routed their enemy. Tho' the affair was but of short duration, the Brigade lost four hundred men, of which two hundred were of the 40th; the loss of officers was also very great; we had eight wounded, among whom my two Messmates, the Lieut.-Col. and Major, were severely handled: it was one of the most painful days of my Life.[105]

Soon afterwards, before the British gun batteries had made

progress against the French defences, news reached Marshal Beresford that Soult was marching from Andalucia at the head of an army of nearly 25,000 men. The French Marshal's hastily assembled force included a very strong and effective cavalry contingent of over 4,000 sabres.

Wellington had expected Soult to attempt the relief of Badajoz and had left very specific instructions for Beresford on whether to give battle or not:

> Marshal Beresford will consider of and decide upon the chance of success, according to a view of the relative number of both armies, and making a reasonable allowance for the number of Spanish troops which will co-operate with him.... If he should think his strength sufficient to fight a general action to save the siege of Badajoz, he will collect his troops to fight it. I believe that, upon the whole, the most central and advantageous place to collect the troops will be at Albuera. . .All this must of course be left to the decision of Sir William Beresford. I authorize him to fight the action if he should think proper, or to retire if he should not.[106]

With his own British and Portuguese troops, plus around 14,000 Spanish under his command, Beresford decided he had sufficient force to block Soult's advance and engage him in battle. He quickly ordered an end to the siege, sending the guns and supplies back to Elvas and marching most of his troops south along the road to the village of Albuera.

THE ALLIED ARMY CONCENTRATES

The small Spanish village of Albuera is 16 miles southeast of Badajoz and straddles important cross-roads. One route it covers is the main road from Seville to Badajoz – and it was along this route Soult's army was rapidly advancing. A small river flows through the village, but it is not deep and its banks, particularly on the south side of the village, offer no major hindrance. The countryside around is predominantly rolling fields, with the only feature of note being a gentle sloping ridge that runs north to south. While this feature allowed the Allies to take the high ground, it was not a significant obstacle such as that at Bussaco. The entire southern end of the battlefield was good cavalry country – an observation that will prove incredibly important during the battle.

Early in the afternoon of the 15th of May, Major General William Stewart's 2nd Division and Hamilton's Portuguese Division reached the village of Albuera, followed closely by Sir Charles Alten's Brigade of the King's German Legion. Major General Lowry Cole's 4th Division was still outside Badajoz, covering the removal of the artillery and stores, but they were expected to join as soon as possible. Fourteen thousand Spaniards were also on their way, comprising soldiers from various commands, including those of generals Blake and Castaños. The Spanish, individually brave, were notoriously bad at manoeuvring in the face of the enemy, and in previous combined Allied operations had proven to be unreliable.

Beresford, expecting a direct French attack along the road towards the village, placed two battalions of the King's German Legion inside Albuera and positioned the 2nd Division to block the road behind them. Tasked with holding the left flank were the Portuguese Division, while the Spanish were placed on the heights to the right – Beresford considered his right flank to be Soult's least likely point of attack.

The logistics of concentrating the various units in the right place and on time were very difficult. The Spanish only arrived in the middle of the night in dribs and drabs, meaning that the first hours of daylight on the 16th were spent trying to organise them and direct them into the correct position – they were only formed into line an hour before the battle began.

Likewise, the British 4th Division only arrived at dawn, and even then, they were missing nearly all their 2nd Brigade under Lieutenant Colonel Kemmis. The 2nd Brigade had been stranded on the opposite bank of the Guadiana River after it rose suddenly and were forced to take a huge detour via the town of Elvas. It was not known when they would eventually reach the field of battle. To make matters worse, those troops of the 4th Division that had arrived were exhausted and hungry.

SOULT'S OPENING MOVES

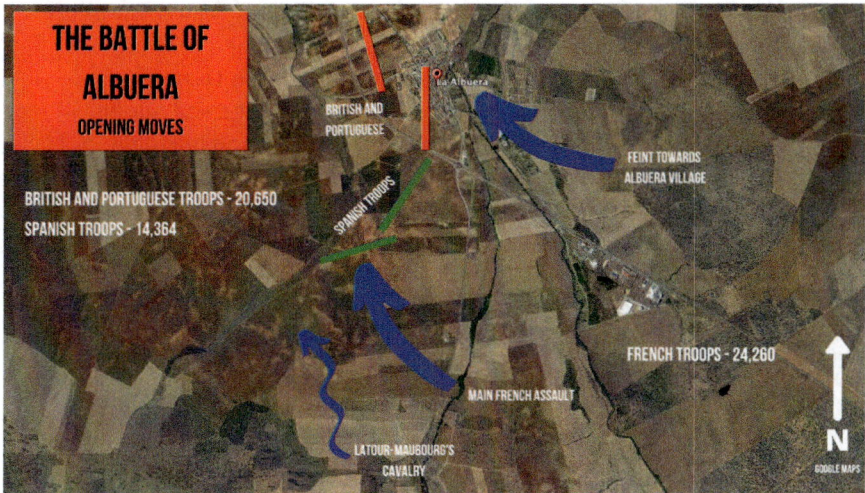

THE BATTLE OF ALBUERA
OPENING MOVES

BRITISH AND PORTUGUESE TROOPS - 20,650
SPANISH TROOPS - 14,364

BRITISH AND PORTUGUESE

SPANISH TROOPS

FEINT TOWARDS ALBUERA VILLAGE

FRENCH TROOPS - 24,260

MAIN FRENCH ASSAULT

LATOUR-MAUBOURG'S CAVALRY

N

GOOGLE MAPS

The French plan of attack was a good one. Marshal Soult had no intention of flinging the bulk of his infantry against the village (as Masséna had done at Fuentes de Oñoro). Instead, he sent a small, but vigorous, diversionary attack against Albuera while executing a powerful left hook against the Allied right flank. Soult later claimed that he was not aware that the Spanish had already arrived on the field of battle. But this claim seems unlikely given the amount of noise the Spanish contingent would have made arriving in the middle of the night, and that they had still been forming up well after daybreak.

The morning of the 16th of May 1811 was dull and overcast with intermittent showers. Lieutenant Charles Leslie of the 29th Regiment of Foot later recalled the opening moves of the battle:

> The whole were drawn up as for a grand parade, in full view of the enemy, so that Soult could see almost every man, and he was also enabled to choose his point of attack; which would not have

been the case if we had been kept under cover a few yards farther back, behind the crest of the heights, or had been made to lie down, as we used to do under the Duke of Wellington. That part of the 4th Division under Sir Lowry Cole, which had just arrived from Badajoz, were posted in second line in our rear. Before we had time to halt in our position, we observed two large columns of the enemy, supported by cavalry and artillery, moving towards the bridge and village of Albuera, which was occupied by the light corps of the German Legion. . .the first attack here commenced, under cover of a heavy cannonade, upon the village and our line in its rear. The Germans made a gallant defence, and maintained their post; but as the enemy apparently seemed to make a push at this point, [Lieutenant Colonel John] Colborne's brigade was ordered to move down in support of the troops in the village. Soult must have been much delighted on observing this movement: it, no doubt, was precisely what he most wished; because the columns which appeared to threaten the village and our line was only a ruse to distract our attention and neutralise the English force which he most dreaded. Our skillful adversary was, in the meantime, throwing his masses directly across our right flank. . .and it was with no small surprise that we most unexpectedly heard a sharp fire commence in that quarter. The error our chief had been led into now became evident.[107]

What Leslie could hear was two French infantry divisions, over 8,000 men, emerging from behind the cover of trees to confront a thin line of Spaniards – four battalions of the Spanish 4th Division under the command of General José Pascual de Zayas y Chacón – usually referred to as General Zayas. Beresford had requested that General Blake send more men to support Zayas, but the proud Spaniard had declined, still believing that the main French assault was against the village and that the move against his flank was a feint. Thus, once a sudden squall of rain had stopped, and the French steamroller struck, Zayas was on his own.

The Spanish army is often derided in British accounts of the war, but despite their lack of training, poor equipment, and the shortcomings of their commanders, the average Spaniard was tough and more than willing to fight the French time and again. At Albuera, Zayas's division showed exceptional bravery and tenacity. The huge

French columns advanced methodically towards them with their battle cries of *'Vive l'Empereur'* and *'En Avant.'* The Spanish held their ground and let rip with a brutal volley that inflicted heavy casualties. French General Jean-Baptiste Girard then made the fatal error of halting his men to return fire. Chaos ensued as both armies stood pounding each other from close range.

Beresford, realising that the Spanish could be broken at any minute and the Allied flank rolled up, commanded Major General William Stewart's 2nd Division to redeploy to support their ally. Stewart ordered his men forward at the double. Amongst them was the 29th and our old friend Charles Lesley:

> We were suddenly thrown into open column, and moved rapidly along the heights to our right flank for nearly a mile under a tremendous cannonade, for the French had already established themselves on some commanding heights, which raked us as we advanced, Captain Humphrey and several men being killed.[108]

Moyle Sherer was also present with the division's 3rd Brigade and recalled:

> I remember well, as we moved down in column, shot and shell flew over and through it in quick succession; we sustained little injury from either, but a captain of the 29th [presumably Captain Humphrey mentioned by Leslie in the above quote] had been dreadfully lacerated by a ball, and lay directly in our path. We passed close to him, and he knew us all; and the heart-rending tone in which he called to us for water, or to kill him, I shall never forget. He lay alone, and we were in motion, and could give him no succour; for on this trying day, such of the wounded that could not walk lay unattended where they fell — all was hurry and struggle. . .When we arrived near the discomfited and retiring Spaniards, and formed our line to advance through them towards the enemy, a very noble looking young Spanish officer rode up to me and, and begged me, with a sort of proud and brave anxiety, to explain to the English, that his countrymen were ordered to retire, but were not flying.[109]

Lieutenant Colonel John Colborne's 1st Brigade (comprising the 1/3rd Regiment of Foot aka the Buffs, 2/31st, 2/48th and the 2/66th) marched out past the flank of the retiring Spanish and then deployed into line formation – allowing them to bring the maximum number of muskets to bear on the French. Amongst the officers' present was Major William Brooke of the 2/48th Regiment, who later wrote:

> The British line deployed, halted, and fired two rounds: the heads of the French columns returned the fire three-deep, the front-rank kneeling. Finding these columns were not to be shaken by fire, the three leading battalions of the brigade prepared to charge with the bayonet, by the order of Major General the Hon. William Stewart, who led them on in person to the attack in the most gallant manor. The charge being delivered, the French. . .gave way.[110]

But despite this initial success, General Stewart, no doubt brave and aggressive, had made a terrible tactical blunder. The decision to form line was about to lead to what was arguably the biggest British disaster of the Peninsular War.

CATASTROPHE – THE DESTRUCTION OF COLBORNE'S BRIGADE

The line of Colborne's Brigade rippled with volley-fire as it advanced against the exposed left flank of the nearest French column. It seemed likely that the bluecoats must give way under such an intense hail of bullets. But in the confusion, on a battlefield thick with smoke and rain, the British officers failed to notice a deadly threat.

In the distance, watching the battle develop, was General Victor de Fay de Latour-Maubourg. He was an experienced officer and had served under Napoleon himself in Egypt and at Austerlitz and Friedland. At Albuera he commanded the French cavalry – a large force that included several crack regiments. As he skirted the French left flank, he observed with surprise as the British moved forward in line – leaving their flanks and rear completely exposed. Realising that he needed to act, and seeing that the retiring French infantry columns were in danger, he ordered his nearest cavalry regiments to attack. At the forefront were the 1st Lancers of the Vistula Legion – a mounted unit made up mainly of Polish volunteers. Alongside them were the

2nd Hussars and possibly other units.

The Polish horsemen, clad in their distinctive *Czapka* headgear with their blue jackets and yellow facings, slowly gathered speed as they came around behind the Buffs. Suddenly the charge was sounded. The men dipped their lances and struck the thin line of red.

The next few minutes were complete chaos for the redcoats. Understanding too late that they had made a terrible mistake, some tried to run, others lay on the floor playing dead, while the majority quickly formed themselves into rally squares. These impromptu squares were little more than disorganised huddles, incapable of keeping back the long, deadly lances of the Vistula Legion.

Lieutenant John Clarke, of the 66th wrote:

> Our men now ran into groups of six or eight, to do as best they could; the officers snatched up muskets and joined them, determined to sell their lives dearly. Quarter was not asked, and rarely given. Poor Colonel Waller, of the Quarter-Master-General's staff, was cut down close to me; he put up his hands asking for quarter, but the ruffian cut his fingers off. My Ensign, Hay, was run through the lungs by a lance which came out of his back; he fell but got up again. The Lancer delivered another thrust, the lance striking Hay's breast-bone; down he went, and the Pole rolled over in the mud beside him.[111]

Major Brooke was also in the forefront of this brutal fight, and later wrote of his experience, and the cruelty of the polish Lancers:

> The French cavalry that had been judiciously posted on the left rear of their heavy column, took advantage of our brigade being unsupported, galloped around the hill. . .and coming into the rear of our unfortunate battalion cut them off. Two squadrons of our 4th Dragoons were despatched by General Lumley for the purpose of giving us assistance: but they only shared the same fate as our infantry. . .The 31st Regiment, the left battalion of our brigade, alone escaped: it was still at the foot of the hill in solid column, not having had time to deploy along with the 3rd, 66th and 48th. Part of the victorious French cavalry were Polish Lancers: from the conduct of this regiment on the field of action I believe many of them to have been intoxicated, as they rode over the wounded, barbarously darting their lances into them.

Several unfortunate prisoners were killed in this manner, while being led from the field to the rear of the enemy's lines. . .I was being led as a prisoner between two French infantry soldiers when one of these lancers rode up, and deliberately cut me down. Then, taking the skirts of my regimental coat, he endeavoured to pull it over my head. Not satisfied with this brutality, the wretch tried by every means in his power to make his horse trample on me, by dragging me along the ground and wheeling his horse over my body.[112]

Thankfully for the confused Major, the lancer's horse was kinder than its master and refused to hurt him.

The lancers, sweeping across the southern portion of the battlefield, even attacked Marshal Beresford and his staff. Beresford, a sturdy, well-built man, parried a lance-thrust and unhorsed his assailant using brute strength.

As Colborne's Brigade was overrun and destroyed, several colours were also lost. A British regiment's colours, also known as standards, are the heart and soul of the unit and embody their history and traditions – to lose them is considered a terrible disgrace. The actual number of captured colours has been debated extensively. The French claimed to have captured six (the figure used by historian Charles Oman in his chapter on the battle), but the truth seems somewhat more complicated. Both colours of the 2/48th and the 2/66th were certainly captured, and at one point so was the regimental colour of the Buffs, but it was recovered later in the day by a sergeant of the 1/7th Fusiliers. The King's colour was saved by Lieutenant Matthew Latham who tore it from its staff and stuffed it inside his tunic. He lost an arm and his nose in the battle to protect it, but against all odds he survived and was forever a hero to the men of the Buffs.

A FIREFIGHT LIKE NO OTHER

Despite the destruction of Colborne's Brigade, the rest of the 2nd Division continued to stand in front of the huge French columns exchanging brutal volleys with them. Oman calls this 'the hardest and most splendid fighting done that day.'[113] Lieutenant Charles Leslie picks up the story:

> This was the moment at which the murderous and desperate battle really began. A most overwhelming fire of artillery and small arms was opened upon us, which was vigorously returned. There we unflinchingly stood, and there we fell: our ranks were at some places swept away by sections. This dreadful contest had continued for some time, when an officer of artillery – I believe a German – came up and said he had brought two or three guns, but that he could find no one to give him orders, our superior officers being all wounded or killed. It was suggested that he could not do wrong in opening directly on the enemy, which was accordingly done. Our line at length became so reduced that it resembled a chain of skirmishers in extended order; while, from the necessity of closing in towards the colours, and our numbers fast diminishing, our right flank became still further exposed. The enemy, however, did not avail himself of the advantage which this circumstance might have afforded him. We continued to maintain this unprecedented conflict with unabated energy. The enemy, notwithstanding his superiority of numbers, had not obtained one inch of ground.[114]

Near to Leslie stood Moyle Sherer:

> This murderous contest of musketry lasted long. We were the whole time progressively advancing upon and shaking the enemy. . .To describe my feelings throughout this wild scene with fidelity, would be impossible: at intervals, a shriek or a groan told that men were falling around me; but it was not always that the tumult of the contest suffered me to catch these sounds. A constant feeling to the centre of the line, and the gradual diminution of our front, more truly bespoke the havoc of death. As we moved though slowly, yet ever a little in advance, our own killed and wounded lay behind us; but we arrived among those of the enemy, and those of the Spaniards who had fallen in the onset: we trod among the dead and dying, all reckless of them. But how shall I picture the British soldier going into action? He is neither heated by brandy, stimulated by the hope of plunder, or inflamed by the deadly feelings of revenge; he does not even indulge in expressions of animosity against his foes; he moves forward confident of victory, never dreams of the possibility of

defeat, and braves death with all the accompanying horrors. . .with the most cheerful intrepidity.[115]

The nature of the fighting is showed by the fact that the King's colour of the 57th Regiment of Foot received 17 shots through it and the Regimental colour was pierced 21 times during the firefight.[116] Casualties were horrific, but we will return to the numbers at the end of the chapter.

ATTACK OF THE 4TH DIVISION

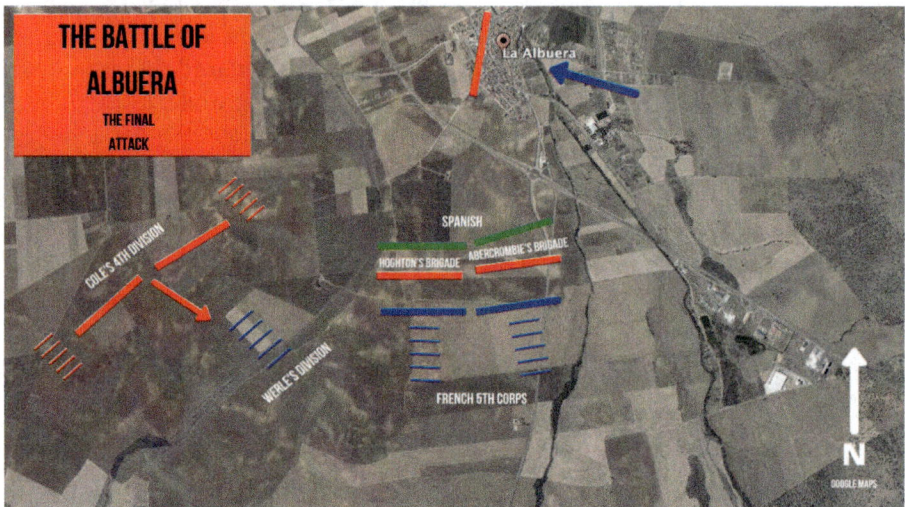

At this point in the battle, the rival commanders were both missing in action. Marshal Soult, usually a gifted strategist, was standing idly by while the bulk of his infantry, formed in column, were being ripped to shreds in a vicious musketry dual. While Beresford, inexplicably, had left the main point of action to scour the left flank of the battlefield in person for Hamilton's Portuguese Division, which it seems could not be found because of the poor visibility. Therefore, the decisive moment of the battle was brought about by a young Lieutenant Colonel of the Portuguese army – Henry Hardinge. Hardinge, who would one day become a Field marshal, rode over to Major General Lowry Cole, commanding the 4th Division, and urged him to attack the French and relieve what remained of the 2nd Division before they were broken. Cole was under strict instructions not to move – his division was tasked with protecting the rear and keeping the road to Juromenha open. The General, a tough and experienced Irishman, considered his options for a moment and then made the decisive decision to attack. It was around 1 p.m.

The movement was not without significant risk – Latour-Maubourg's cavalry were still in the vicinity and keen for another opportunity for glory. Cole, determined not to make the same mistake as Stewart, moved his division in battalion columns that were echeloned from left to right (i.e. staggered). He placed a square comprising light companies on his right flank and the Portuguese Loyal Lusitanian Legion on the left. He also made sure that the Allied cavalry would be available to cover his flanks as best as they were able. It was a difficult manoeuvre, but the division executed it perfectly.

Soult, seeing the danger that Cole's advance represented, finally emerged from his lethargy, and sent his reserves to stop the 4th Division. General François Werlé's 6,000 men deployed in three columns to meet the Redcoats. Sergeant John Spencer Cooper of the 2/7th Royal Fusiliers was in the thick of the action:

> Having arrived at the foot of the hill, we began to climb its slope with panting breath, while the roll and thunder of furious battle increased. Under the tremendous fire of the enemy our thin line staggers, and men are knocked about like skittle; but not a step backward is taken. Here our Colonel and all the field-officers of the brigade fell killed or wounded, but no confusion ensued. The orders were, 'Close up'; 'Close in'; 'Fire away'; 'Forward.' This is done. We are close to the enemy's columns; they break and rush down the other side of the hill in the greatest mob-like confusion. In a minute or two, our nine pounders and light infantry gain the summit, and join in sending a shower of iron and lead into the broken mass. We followed down the slope firing and huzzaring, till recalled by the bugle.[117]

While Sergeant Cooper's description is vivid, it compresses an epic and prolonged musketry duel into a single sentence. In fact, before Werlé's troops finally broke, the two sides stood almost muzzle to muzzle for nearly half an hour, exchanging volleys at point blank range. Nearly all the 4th Division's senior officers, including General Cole, became casualties. Eventually, the French were broken. Werlé had had more men, but he failed to redeploy them from column into line and thus could bring fewer muskets to bear – a classic Peninsular War scenario.

For all intents and purposes, the battle was now over. Under a heavy, drenching rain, covered by their cavalry and artillery, the French withdrew back to their bivouac. Both commanding officers seemed unwilling to continue the fight – shocked at the slaughter they had witnessed. Beresford and his battered army had held their ground, Soult's attempt to relieve Badajoz had failed, and late the next day the French began withdrawing to Seville. It was a British victory, but one won at a terrible cost.

Sergeant Cooper described the aftermath of the battle:

Having returned to the top of the ridge we piled arms and looked about. What a scene! The dead and wounded lying all around. In some places the dead were in heaps. One of these was nearly three feet high, but I did not count the number in it. When our regiment was mustered after the battle it numbered about 80. As we went into fire 435 strong, we lost 355. The first battalion some hundreds stronger than ours lost 353. All the three colonels of our brigade fell on that hillside; viz., Colonel Sir William Myers, killed; Colonels Edward Blakeney and Ellis, wounded. What was now to be done with the wounded that were so thickly strewed on every side? The town of Albuhera [sic] had been totally unroofed and unfloored for firewood by the enemy, and there was no other town within several miles; besides the rain was pouring down, and the poor sufferers were as numerous as the unhurt. To be short, the wounded that could not walk were carried in blankets to the bottom of the bloody hill, and laid among the wet grass. Whether they had any orderlies to wait on them, or how many lived or died, I can't tell. . .We were wet, weary, and dirty; without food or shelter. Respecting the wounded, General Blake, the Spanish Commander, was asked to help us with them, but he refused to send any men to carry them off.[118]

Moyle Sherer, a gifted writer, captures the awful scene that he witnessed:

> The roar of the battle is hushed; the hurry of action is over; let us walk over the corpse-encumbered field. Look around – behold thousands of slain, thousands of wounded, writhing with anguish, and groaning with agony and despair. Move a little this way, here lie four officers of the French hundredth, all corpses. How beautiful, how serene a countenance! Perhaps, on the banks of the Loire, some mother thinks anxiously of her darling child. Here fought the 3rd Brigade, here the Fusiliers: how thick these heroes lie! Most of the bodies are already stripped; rank is no longer distinguished. . .Here charged the Polish Lancers; not long ago, the trampling of horses, the shout, the cry, the prayer, the death-stroke, all mingled their wild sounds on this spot. . .Here again lie headless trunks, and bodies torn and struck down by cannon shot; such a death is sudden, horrid, but 'tis merciful. . .Some readers will call this scene romantic, others disgusting: no matter; it is faithful; and it would be well for kings and politicians, and generals, if, while they talk of victories with exultation, and of defeats with philosophical indifference, they would allow their fancies to wander to the theatre of war, and the field of carnage.[119]

CASUALTIES

While there were other battles in the Peninsular War with heavier overall casualties, such as Talavera, the Battle of Albuera was the bloodiest in proportion to the numbers engaged. The British lost 4,159 men killed wounded and captured, the Portuguese 389, the Spaniards 1,368. The French suffered just as heavily, with just under 6,000 casualties. But numbers without context tell us nothing. It is only when you compare them to the amount of men involved that the full horror becomes apparent.

While the exact percentage varies between studies, it is commonly understood in the military that once a unit suffers over 30% casualties, it rapidly loses cohesion and is no longer effective. At

Albuera, the total Allied losses amounted to just under 17%. But for the British, the casualties were closer to 50%. Colborne's Brigade, caught in the open by Latour-Maubourg's cavalry, suffered a 68% casualty rate, losing a staggering 1,413 men out of 2,066. Among this brigade was the 1/3rd Buffs who lost 643 men – 85% of the unit. Moyle Sherer's battalion, the 2/34th, in the same division, was let off lightly and *only* suffered 128 casualties – a number that is still over 20% of the entire unit strength. The Fusilier Brigade of the 4th Division (of which Sergeant Cooper was a part), who made the decisive final assault against the French reserves, lost 1,045 – just over 50% of their number.

While the British had borne the brunt of the fighting, Zayas's Spanish Division had also played an important role and suffered heavily for their bravery – 681 casualties out of a total strength of 4,882 (14%).

The French were also well and truly battered. Overall, Soult's force lost 25% of its men killed, wounded, or captured. The 34th Line Regiment of Girard's Division, which stood toe to toe with the Spanish and British throughout most of the day, had 43% casualties, and the 12th Léger in Werlé's Reserve Brigade took 769 casualties – 35% of those present.[120]

Marshal Beresford had struggled with the pressure of commanding a large army in a major engagement against an experienced French commander like Soult. He had won the battle but at an enormous cost. The British politicians were also shocked by the slaughter, Wellington's older brother, William, wrote:

> Beresford's action is considered here as a proof of the astonishing bravery of the British troops, which appears to have saved him and his army- there are so many letters from the army detailing particulars that every body knows the whole story, even to the General's loss of Head and ordering the retreat etc. Of course I have been cautious in saying a word, but it should be supposed that any friend of yours to depreciate the merit of any general. But the truth is Beresford has entirely lost all hope of being considered by us lookers on as general.[121]

Shaken by the nature of the victory, Beresford now marched his army back to Badajoz – it was time to begin another siege.

CHAPTER SEVEN: THE SECOND SIEGE OF BADAJOZ

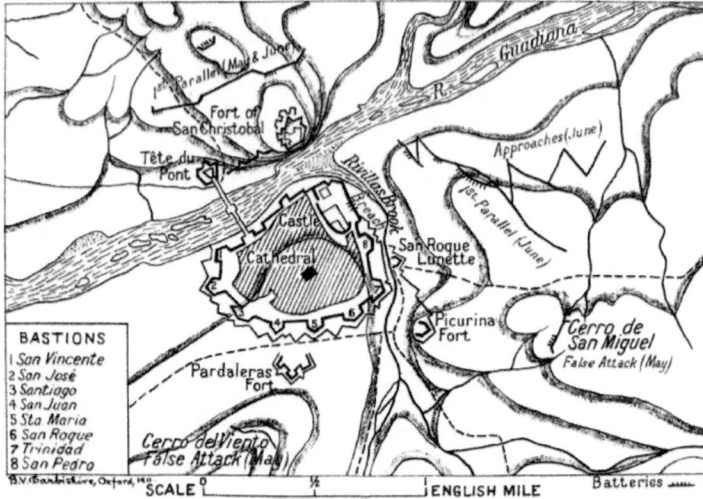

THE FIRST AND SECOND SIEGE OF BADAJOZ
MAP ORIGINALLY PUBLISHED IN OMAN, CHARLES, A HISTORY OF THE PENINSULAR WAR, VOLUME FOUR, (CLARENDON PRESS, 1911).

With Soult's battered army forced to retire after Albuera, and the French Army of Portugal in a similar state after their drubbing at Fuentes de Oñoro, Wellington had a small window of opportunity to redeploy some of his divisions and take another crack at Badajoz. The French, lacking an overall commander in Spain, were disjointed and their marshals jealous of one another – this made it difficult for them to concentrate their armies and make the most of their superior numbers.

Wellington's 3rd and 7th Divisions, marched south to bolster the besieging army that Wellington himself was now to command. Marshal Beresford, perhaps suffering from what we would call Post Traumatic Stress Disorder, had been discretely posted back to Portugal to continue his excellent work rebuilding the Portuguese army. In his stead came General Rowland Hill, who had finally recovered from his illness and returned to the Peninsular. He was a steady hand and was immediately tasked with commanding the blocking force south of Badajoz, whose task was to cover any fresh relief attempt by Marshal Soult.

Wellington's biggest weakness was that he still lacked a powerful siege train. He had more guns than Marshal Beresford had gathered during the first siege, but the majority were still obsolete and not fit for purpose. There were 30 24-pounders and four 16-pounder guns, as well as eight 8-inch and four 10-inch howitzers.[122] The old brass guns had irregular calibres and would warp when they were hot. As well as suitable artillery, the Allied army also lacked sufficient engineering officers. Those that they did have lacked experience in large siege operations.

On the 25th of May, Major General Houston's 7th Division began the investment of the city. They took up position on the right of the Guadiana River opposite Fort San Cristoval. They were followed two days later by Picton's 3rd Division and Hamilton's Portuguese Division, which were positioned to the east of the city, opposite the castle. Yet again, the British planned to focus their attention on the two most powerful points of the city's defences. It was felt that if either of them could be captured, then the rest of the city would be forced to surrender.

THE DIGGING BEGINS

On the night of the 30th of May, 1,600 men of the 3rd Division began digging their zigzag trenches towards the castle. Our old friend William Grattan, of the 88th Connaught Rangers, was with them:

> This was my first siege, and the novelty of the thing compensated me in some degree for the sleepless nights I used to pass at its commencement; but habit soon reconciled me, and I could sleep soundly in a battery for a couple of hours at a time. Nothing astonished me so much as the noise made by the engineers; I expected that their loud talking would bring the enemy's attention towards the sound of our pick-axes, and that all the cannon in the town would be turned against us—and, in short, I thought every moment would be my last. I scarcely ventured to

breathe until we had completed a respectable first parallel, and when it was fairly finished, just as morning began to dawn, I felt inexpressibly relieved. The 7th Division was equally fortunate before San Christoval. As soon as the enemy had a distinct view of what we had been doing, he opened a battery or two against us, with, however, but little effect, and I began to think a siege was not that tremendous thing I had been taught to expect; but at this moment a thirty-two pound shot passed through a mound of earth in front of that part of the parallel in which I was standing (which was but imperfectly finished), and taking two poor fellows of the 83rd (who were carrying a hand-barrow) across their bellies, cut them in two, and whirled their remnants through the air. I had never before so close a view of the execution a round shot was capable of performing, and it was of essential service to me during this and my other sieges. It was full a week afterwards before I held myself as upright as before.[123]

Private William Wheeler, of the 51st Regiment of Foot, who we last met at the Battle of Fuentes de Oñoro, was with the 7th Division, opposite Fort San Cristoval, he later wrote home:

Fort San Cristoval is an out work of great strength, close to the garrison, but is separated from it by the river, its communication is by a bridge. It is against this Fort we are throwing up our works. Under the cover of night we commence throwing up any new work, as soon as the enemy hear our pick axes they give us a light by throwing out a quantity of fireballs. This would be very accommodating on their part if they did not open as many guns as they can bring to bear on the place. These balls give a great light around the place where they fall and enables them to point their guns with great precision. The other night we began to break ground in a fresh place, they very politely gave us a light by sending out six beautiful fireballs, the word 'down' was given, but before we had time to stretch ourselves on Mother Earth, they discharged a volley of round and grapeshot. One of the round-shot must have passed pretty near my cranium, I thought I was wounded, my head ached violently. I felt the pain a long time, and it was with difficulty I could perform my duty. Had I been working in a place where there was no danger I should have given up, but here I was ashamed to complain, lest any of my comrades should laugh at me.[124]

He goes on to give an excellent description of the weather and the difficulties faced by the redcoats as the siege got underway:

It is astonishing with what rapidity our work advances, in a short time we had four batteries ready. When off duty, in our camp we are exposed to the scorching heat of the sun, we have no tents, not a tree or bush to shelter us, we have to fetch every drop of water we use at the distance of three miles, we must be ready at a moment's notice should the enemy sally. . . The day our batteries opened on Fort San Cristoval I was on covering party and stationed in the trench in front of No. 4 battery. The first hour the shock of the guns would almost lift us off the ground, but we soon became so used to it that we could sleep as comfortable as if we had been in a featherbed. The duty in the trenches by day is very fatiguing, almost suffocated for the want of air and nearly baked by the sun, parching with thirst, with a beautiful river close to us but it might as well be 100 miles off – for if anyone only indulged the eye with a peep, bang goes half a dozen musket at his head. Then we are kept in constant motion by swarms of flies to say nothing of the vermin that has stationed themselves inside our clothes, who are as busy as possible laying siege to our bodies, while we cannot bring a finger to bear on them.[125]

On the morning of the 3rd of June, the Allied batteries were in position and opened fire. The guns, unsurprisingly, were inaccurate and those firing at the castle were too far out for maximum effectiveness. In siege warfare, artillery accuracy is of the utmost importance, as the round-shot need to strike their target in exactly the same place repeatedly to create a breach that the infantry can then storm. The French counter-battery fire was also successful as Private Wheeler witnessed:

Yesterday about midday I was in the trench in front of No. 2 Battery. An old Portuguese had just arrived with a car loaded with ammunition drawn by two oxen, he had just got repeatedlyhis load deposited in the magazine when the enemy favoured us with a shell from the 'Big Tom of Lincoln' (the name we have given to one of their tremendous mortars). I watched its progress and saw it burst a few feet over the oxen, they were cut to pieces with the car. When the cloud of dust and smoke cleared away we observed the old fellow running like a deer, he had miraculously escaped unhurt. Besides killing the oxen, one of our guns in the battery was dismounted. Another was soon mounted, but it caused some trouble as they dapped another shell into the battery and wounded several men.[126]

ATTACK ON FORT CRISTOVAL

On the 6th of June, the breach in the wall of Fort San Cristoval was judged by Lieutenant Forster of the Royal Engineers to be *'practicable.'* A storming party of the 7th Division was quickly organised. Attacks against breaches were notoriously dangerous, and so it was the standard procedure to ask for volunteers to form a 'Forlorn Hope' – these brave men would be the tip of the spear, leading the attack and drawing the enemy fire.

At midnight, Ensign Joseph Dyas, a popular Irish officer of the 51st Regiment of Foot, accompanied by Lieutenant Forster and 25 men, advanced silently towards the breach. What they didn't realise was that the French engineers had used the cover of darkness to clear much of the breach and plant a dangerous variety of obstructions to greet the Allied assault troops.

Following close behind the Forlorn Hope was a storming party commanded by Major Macintosh of the 85th Foot. Private Wheeler was with them:

> In the evening we advanced towards the fort but lay hid until the shades of night had cast her mantle over us, then moved on towards the breach observing the strictest silence. To divert the attention of the enemy all our guns were opened on the fort, but the French commandant was not to be duped, the sly old fox had anticipated our visit and had prepared everything to give us a warm reception. Each man in the fort was provided with six loaded firelocks. Live shells were placed so as to be rolled into the trench. In short, nothing that would annoy us was forgotten. We advanced up the glacis close to the walls. Not a head was to be seen above the walls, and we began to think the enemy had retired into the town. We entered the trench and fixed our ladders, when, sudden as a flash of lightning, the whole place was in a blaze. It will be impossible for me to describe to you what

followed. You can better conceive it by figuring to your mind's eye a deep trench or ditch filled with men who are endeavouring to mount the wall by means of ladders. The top of this wall crowded with men hurling down shells and hand grenades on the heads of them below, and when all these are expended, they have each six or seven loaded firelocks which they discharge into the trenches quick as possible. Add to this some half dozen cannon scouring the trench with grape. That will immediately present to your imagination the following frightful picture. Heaps of brave fellows killed and wounded, ladders shot to pieces, and falling together with the men down upon the living and dead.[127]

Lieutenant Grattan, who wasn't personally involved in the attack but was nearby, added:

Some of the foremost succeeded in planting ladders against its rugged face, but their efforts were baffled by the exertions of the French engineers who, notwithstanding our fire of grape and musketry, had contrived to clear away the rubbish from the base of the wall; and the ladders were in consequence not of a sufficient length to enable the men to make a lodgement. A quarter of an hour had now elapsed, during which time several fruitless attempts had been made to enter the fort; and Major Macintosh, with his few remaining men, succeeded with difficulty in reaching their own lines, which they had left but a short time before with feelings of a very different description. None of the party could give any account of Ensign Dyas—indeed, how could they? For the storming party had never seen the Forlorn Hope from the moment they descended the ditch! It was a generally received opinion that Dyas had fallen. Major Macintosh, in company with a few friends, was sitting in his tent talking over the failure of the attack, and regretting, amongst others, the loss of this officer, when to his amazement he entered the tent not only alive but unhurt. This brave young fellow, after having lost the greater part of his men, and finding himself unsupported by the storming party, at length quitted the ditch, but not until he heard the enemy entering it by the sally-port.[128]

The attack had been a failure. The number of soldiers involved was far too small to force the breach, the ladders were not long enough, and the French had been given too much time between the creation of the breach and the assault to better prepare their defence. The attacking force lost 92 men dead and wounded from 180 that were engaged.[129]

The following morning, the bombardment began again. Seven iron 24-pound guns that had been brought forward from Lisbon began a heavy fire against the walls of the castle. Despite the heavier calibre and better accuracy, these new guns still couldn't batter a sufficient breach in the castle and so Wellington and his engineers determined that they would have to attack Fort San Cristoval once again. The fort had taken a drubbing since the start of the siege, but its defences were still strong, as the historian Charles Oman explains:

> Here there were now two breaches, a large and a small one; the parapets were completely knocked to pieces, and the fort looked a mere battered heap; its fire had been nearly silenced—so much so that not a single casualty occurred in the trench before it during the last twelve hours of bombardment. Nevertheless, the breaches were not very practicable, for here (as at the castle) the garrison had, by hard work during the nights, cleared away great part of the *débris* below the breach; they could not be prevented from doing so, because the besiegers' batteries were so far away that they were unable to command the dead ground in the bottom of the ditch. On each morning the battered parapet was found to have been replaced with sandbags and wool-packs, and the breach itself stopped with *chevaux de fries* [sword blades mounted on a portable barrier]. These were swept away again by continual battering, both on the 8th and the 9th, but the gallant garrison began to replace them on each evening the moment that dusk fell. Nor could this be prevented, because, contrary to all the rules of siegecraft, the besiegers had not sapped up close enough to the walls to enable them to prevent repairs from being carried out. General Phillipon had doubled the garrison of the fort, which now consisted of two companies instead of the one that had held it on the 6th. The men were furnished with three muskets each, and a great store of grenades, fire-balls, and live shell, prepared for throwing by hand, had been sent up into the work.[130]

ANOTHER ASSAULT

On the night of the 9th of June, General Houston's 7th Division prepared to attack again. This time they would begin their assault earlier, giving the French less opportunity to clear the breaches. Houston also doubled the number of men allocated for the attack, and one hundred of his best marksmen were chosen to give covering fire to the attacking troops. Ensign Dyas, an incredibly brave young officer, volunteered once more to lead the Forlorn Hope. In the book *Soldiers whom Wellington Led*, the author, Edward Fraser, describes how Dyas persuaded General Houston to allow him the honour of leading the assault yet again:

> The Brigadier tried to dissuade him. 'No,' he said, 'you have already done enough. It would be unfair that you should again bear the brunt of this business!' But Ensign Dyas was not to be put off. 'Why, General,' he went on, 'there seemed to be some doubts of the practicability of this business on the last night of our attack. Although I myself don't think the breach is even now practicable, I request you to allow me to lead the party.' Again, the Brigadier refused, and then the Ensign spoke up again. 'General Houston,' he said, 'I hope you won't refuse my request. I am determined, if you order the fort to be stormed fifty times, to lead the advance as long as I have life!' The General was still unwilling for Ensign Dyas to run the risk, but in the end the young officer's earnestness overcame him, and he assented.[131]

Grattan then picks up the story:

> A superior number of troops to those which failed on the 6th, but still *inferior* to the garrison of the fort, were selected for the attack, and the command given to Major McGeechy, an English officer in the service of Portugal, who volunteered this duty— Dyas again leading the Forlorn Hope. As before, the troops advanced under the fire of every gun that could be brought to bear upon them, and with much spirit descended the ditch. A little disorder amongst the men who carried the ladders caused some delay, but the detachment pressed on to the breach without waiting for the reorganisation of the ladder men. The soldiers posted on the glacis, by their determined fire, notwithstanding their exposed situation, forced the enemy to waver, and if ever there was a chance of success, it was at this moment. Dyas and his companions did as much as men could do, but in vain. Their efforts were heroic, though unavailing; the spot

was strewed with the dead and dying; the breach was packed with Frenchmen, and the glacis and ditch covered with our dead and disabled soldiers.[132]

Private Wheeler, of the 51st, was also amongst the assault force for a second time:

> This second attempt was attended with the same ill success as the first. . .the old fox inside was too deep for us. He had caused all the rubbish to be cleared out of the trench. This again placed us just in the same predicament, our ladders were again too short and if possible we received a warmer reception than before. The ladder I was on was broken and down we all came together, men, firelocks, bayonets, in one confused mass, and with us a portion of the wall. After some time the fire slackened, as if the enemy were tired of slaughter, when an officer Lieutenant Westropp came running from the western angle of the Fort calling out to retire –the enemy were entering the trench by the sally port. We then began to leave the trench. Poor Mr Westropp was assisting a wounded man in getting out when he was shot dead just as he had affected his purpose.[133]

The attack had been another bloody failure, costing the small assault force 139 casualties. Despite the incredible efforts of the men, the Fort remained in French hands. The intrepid Ensign Dyas, who had now led two Forlorn Hopes in a short space of time, amazingly survived to tell the tale. He had been wounded in the head and, after the repulse of the assault, had been forced to lie amongst the dead before he was able to make his escape. It is generally considered that any man who led a Forlorn Hope would be immediately promoted, but sadly Ensign Dyas's career was not helped by his immense bravery, as this contemporary poem makes clear:

> I know a man of whom 'tis truly said
> He bravely twice a storming party led,
> And volunteered both times – now here's the rub,
> The gallant fellow still remains a sub.[134]

Eventually, after serving throughout the Peninsular and then at Waterloo, Dyas was promoted to the rank of captain in the Ceylon Regiment. He retired on half-pay in 1822. Though he never achieved the rank and fame he deserved for his deeds, the toast *'To Dyas and the stormers'* was continued by members of King's Own Yorkshire Light Infantry (the descendants of the 51st Regiment of Foot) well into the 20th century.

At midday on the 10th of June, Wellington called together his officers and announced that the siege was to be raised. His intelligence had reported that Marshal Marmont and the 9th Corps, marching south, were soon to combine with Marshal Soult's troops. Wellington, always a realist and sensible with his men's lives, wasn't willing to fight a general action against such a superior enemy that numbered over 50,000 men. Within two days the Allied guns, ammunition and other important stores were on their way to the rear while any material that couldn't be moved was burned. The second siege of Badajoz was now over. Like the first, it had been a complete failure that had achieved very little. There were many reasons for this, including the poor quality of the guns available to the allies, the strength and resolution of the French defenders, the lack of trained British sappers and miners, and the intense time pressures that the Allies were up against to capture the city before it could be relieved. When the two attempts were made to storm Fort San Cristoval not enough men were used. Perhaps if Houston's entire division had attacked at once, forcing the breach and escalading the walls on all sides of the fort, then they may have been successful.

CHAPTER EIGHT: THE END OF THE YEAR

The large battles of 1811 were now finished. Wellington, shifting his army north once more, began a blockade of the border-city of Ciudad Rodrigo. It didn't last long – in September, Marshal Marmont approached the city with over 60,000 men. On the 25th of September, there was a short, sharp clash at the village of El Bodon. A small, Allied force found themselves under attack by 2,500 French cavalry supported by infantry and artillery. Amongst the redcoats that day was Joseph Donaldson of the 94th Regiment of Foot, who later wrote:

> Our position was on a range of heights, over which past the road leading from [Ciudad] Rodrigo to Fuente Guinaldo. Here we lay under arms until about eight o'clock in the morning, when we perceived, issuing out of Rodrigo, one column of cavalry after another, advancing along the road towards our post, to the number of about 40 squadrons; these were succeeded by 12 or 14 battalions of infantry, with twelve pieces of cannon. Our situation now began to get precarious, being completely separated from the rest of the army, by at least 6 miles. Still, we had no orders to retreat and to retreat without orders is not the custom of the British Army. One of the regiments was posted on the hill over which the road passed, and when it was seen that the French were bent upon advancing in that direction, two more regiments, the 77th British, 21st Portuguese and the brigade of cavalry were sent to reinforce them. This was scarcely done, when the advanced squadrons of the enemy's cavalry and artillery made a furious attack on this post, and succeeded in taking two pieces of Portuguese cannon. The Portuguese artillery behaved bravely, having stood until cut down at their guns which were posted on a rising ground to the right. The 5th Regiment was now ordered to charge, and they succeeded in retaking the guns. While this was going on on the right we were attacked by another body of cavalry in front, which was met and repulsed with determined bravery by the 77th regiment. Our cavalry also were warmly engaged, and charged different bodies of the enemy which ascended on the left. Here we kept our post gallantly, surrounded by about 2000 cavalry until at last the French infantry being brought up, we were ordered to retreat in squares on fuente Guinaldo, supported only by the small body of cavalry

already mentioned. The French cavalry seeing us preparing for retreat rushed furiously on, and the various squares were now successively charged by powerful masses of their cavalry, one in particular on three faces of the square, but they halted, and repulsed them with the utmost steadiness and gallantry. The French in those charges suffered severely, having a tremendous fire poured in on them each time. As they rushed on with impetuosity, when they were brought to a dead stop by the points of our bayonets, they were thrown into the greatest confusion, and were brought down by our shot in numbers. The whole now preceded to retreat in excellent order, at an ordinary pace, keeping exact distances, ready to form up in the event of a charge being made we were much annoyed by shot and shell from the heights where the French artillery were posted, some of which falling in the squares did great mischief, killing and wounding several of our men, and blowing up our ammunition. We had about 6 miles to retreat in this manner before we reached the body of the army.[135]

The movement of infantry across the battlefield while formed into battalion square was difficult, but, like the Light Division at the Battle of Fuentes de Oñoro, it was executed brilliantly, and the French cavalry could not break into them. This small and inconclusive battle left the French temporarily in control of the area around Ciudad Rodrigo.

Another battle was fought in October. General Rowland Hill's 2nd Division advanced against the French at Arroyo dos Molinos, north east of Badajoz. It was an excellent victory that destroyed an entire French infantry division and a cavalry brigade. Captain Moyle Sherer of the 34th Regiment of Foot, recalled of the engagement:

We arrived at dusk, on the evening of the 27th, at the village of Alcuescar, distant only four miles from the small town of Arroyo de Molinos [sic], where the division of Gerard slept that night, in fearless but mistaken security. We lay upon our arms, without fires, about six hours; and at two in the morning of the 28th, we moved forward, in profound silence, by a narrow bad road, upon Arroyo de Molinos, near which town we halted, at half-past six, on ground highly favourable both to our formation and concealment. We were here divided into three columns. The first brigade was directed straight forwards on the town; our own, with one of the Portuguese, made a rapid circuitous march to the right of it, and arrived, undercover of fog and rain, within a few yards of the road, by which alone the enemy could retire and on which he was then forming preparatory to his march, in profound ignorance of our approach: our cavalry moved in the centre ready to act as occasion might require. The cheers of the first brigade, which entered the town charging, and bayoneted, drove, or captured his rearguard, first announced to the enemy his imminent and unexpected danger. He would have rapidly retired: in vain; our cavalry galloped forwards, dispersed, sabred, and made prisoners his few horse, who after attempting some formation on the left of the infantry, which stood for a moment in a posture of defence, fled in a great confusion. About 200 yards behind the spot, where the enemy's columns were formed on the plain, rose the rocky and precipitous Sierra de Montanches, and to this, on seeing our brigade advancing rapidly upon them, they ran with unresisting panic. We followed them closely, and scrambling among the rocks, quite mixed with them, and made prisoners at every step.[136]

Like most of Rowland Hill's men, Sherer was a big admirer of his General who they nicknamed 'Daddy':

One thing in our success at Arroyo de Molinos, gratified our division highly; It was a triumph for our general, a triumph all his own. He gained great credit for his well-conducted enterprise, and he gained what, to one of his mild, kind, and humane character, was still more valuable – a solid and bloodless victory; For it is certainly the truest maxim in war, 'that conquest is twice achieved where the achiever brings home full numbers'.[137]

With his army now in a powerful position, Wellington began planning his strategy for 1812. If he wanted to go on the offensive and push into Spain, then the border cities of Ciudad Rodrigo and Badajoz would have to be taken. In preparation, the redcoats, in their winter cantonments, were tasked with making gabions and facines, hundreds of carts were manufactured, bridges were built and, at long last, the heavy siege-guns began their laborious journey from Lisbon. The army would soon be on the move again. . .but that is a story for another day.

This is the end of the main body of The Military History Geek's Guide To...The Peninsular War Volume Two, *but make sure to read the following appendices for more information on the men and battles discussed. Also, please sign up for my mailing list to find out when the next volume of this series will be published –* www.redcoathistory.com/newsletter.

APPENDIX ONE: THE BRITISH ORDER OF BATTLE FOR THE MAIN ENGAGEMENTS

THE BATTLE OF BUSSACO

1st Division: Major General Brent Spencer
1st Brigade, Colonel Edward Stopford:
1/Coldstream Guards, 1/Scots Fusilier Guards, 5/60th (one company)
2nd Brigade, Lieutenant Colonel Lord Blantyre:
2/24th, 1/42nd, 1/61st, 5/60th (one company)
3rd Brigade, Major General von Lowe:
1st KGL Battalion, 2nd KGL Battalion, 5th KGL Battalion, 7th KGL Battalion, Det. KGL Light Battalion
Pakenham's Brigade: 1/7th, 1/79th
Artillery: 1 6pdr Battery

2nd Division: Major General Rowland Hill
1st Brigade, Major General William Stewart:
1/3rd, 2/31st, 2/48th, 2/66th, 5/60th (one company)
2nd Brigade, Colonel William Inglis:
29th, 1/48th, 1/57th, 5/60th (one company)
3rd Brigade, Brigadier General Catlin Craufurd:
2/28th, 2/34th, 2/39th, 5/60th (one company)
Artillery: Portuguese 6pdr Battery and a 9pdr Battery

3rd Division: Major General Thomas Picton
1st Brigade, Colonel Henry MacKinnon:
1/45th, 1/74th, 1/88th
2nd Brigade, Major General Stafford Lightburne:
2/5th, 2/83rd, 5/60th (3 companies)
Portuguese Brigade, Colonel José Champalimaud:
9th Portuguese Line (2 battalions), 21st Portuguese Line (2 battalions)

Artillery: 2 6pdr batteries

4th Division: Major General Lowry Cole
1st Brigade, Brigadier General Alexander Campbell:
2/7th, 1/11th, 2/53rd, 5/60th (one company)
2nd Brigade, Colonel James Kemmis:
3/27th, 1/40th, 97th Foot Regiment, 5/60th (one company)
3rd (Portuguese) Brigade, Colonel Richard Collins:
11th Portuguese Line (2 battalions), 23rd Portuguese Line (2 battalions)

5th Division: Major General James Leith
British Brigade, Lieutenant Colonel James Stevenson Barnes:
3/1st, 1/9th, 2/38th
Portuguese Brigade, Colonel William Spry:
3rd Portuguese Line (2 battalions), 15th Portuguese Line (2 battalions), Thomar Militia Battalion
Portuguese Brigade, Colonel Frederick Eben:
Lusitanian Legion (3 battalions), 8th Portuguese Line (2 battalions)
Artillery: Portuguese 6pdr Battery

Light Division: Brigadier General Robert Craufurd
1st Brigade, Lieutenant Colonel Sidney Beckwith:
1/43rd, 1/95th (4 companies), 3rd Caçadores
2nd Brigade, Lieutenant Colonel Robert Barclay:
1/52nd, 1/95th (4 companies), 1st Caçadores

Portuguese Division: Major General John Hamilton
1st Brigade, Brigadier General Archibald Campbell:
4th Portuguese Line (2 battalions), l0th Portuguese Line (2 battalions)
2nd Brigade, Brigadier General Luiz Fonseca:
2nd Portuguese Line (2 battalions), 14th Portuguese Line (2 battalions)

Independent Portuguese Brigades:

1st Independent Portuguese Brigade, Brigadier General Denis Pack:
1st Portuguese Line (2 battalions), 16th Portuguese Line (2 battalions) 4th Caçadores

5th Independent Portuguese Brigade, Brigadier General Alexander Campbell:
6th Portuguese Line (2 battalions), 18th Portuguese Line (2 battalions), 6th Caçadores

6th Independent Portuguese Brigade, Brigadier General Francis Coleman:
7th Portuguese Line (2 battalions), 19th Portuguese Line (2 battalions), 2nd Caçadores

Cavalry:

4th Dragoons (2 squadrons)

Total artillery was 60 guns

THE BATTLE OF BARROSA

Dilke's Brigade, Brigadier General William Thomas Dilke:
2/1st Foot Guards, 2nd Coldstream Guards (2 companies), 2/3rd Foot Guards (3 companies), 2/95th (2 companies)

Wheatley's Brigade, Brigadier General Henry Wheatley:
1/28th (8 companies), 2/67th, 2/87th

Browne's Flank Battalion, Lieutenant Colonel Browne:
This unit was made up of the flank companies (Grenadier and Light companies) of the 1/9th, 1/28th, 2/82nd

Barnard's Flank Battalion, Colonel Barnard:

2/47th (Light and Grenadier companies), 3/95th (4 companies), 20th Portuguese Line (4 companies)

Cavalry: 2nd Hussars KGL (2 squadrons)

THE BATTLE OF FUENTES DE OÑORO

1st Division: Major General Brent Spencer
1st Brigade, Colonel Edward Stopford:
1/Coldstream Guards, 1/3rd Guards, 5/60th (one company)
2nd Brigade, Major General Miles Nightingall:
2/24th, 2/42nd, 1/79th, 5/60th (one company)
3rd Brigade, Major General Kenneth Alexander Howard:
1/50th, 1/71st, 1/92nd, 5/60th (one company)
4th Brigade, Major General von Lowe:
1st KGL Battalion, 2nd KGL Battalion, 5th KGL Battalion, 7th KGL Battalion, Det. KGL Light Battalion

3rd Division: Major General Thomas Picton
1st Brigade, Colonel Henry MacKinnon:
1/45th, 1/74th, 1/88th, 5/60th (one company)
2nd Brigade, Major General Charles Colville:
2/5th, 2/83rd, 2/88th, 1/94th
Portuguese Brigade, Colonel Manley Power:
9th Portuguese Line (2 battalions), 21st Portuguese Line (2 battalions)

5th Division: Major General Sir William Erskine
1st Brigade, Lieutenant Colonel Andrew Hay:
3/1st, 1/9th, 2/38th, Brunswick Oels (one company)
2nd Brigade, major General James Dunlop:
1/4th, 2/30th, 2/44th, Brunswick Oels (one company)
Portuguese Brigade, Brigadier General William Spry:
3rd Portuguese Line (2 battalions), 15th Portuguese Line (2

battalions), 9th Caçadores

6th Division: Major General Alexander Campbell
1st Brigade, Colonel Richard Hulse:
1/11th, 2/53rd, 1/61st, 5/60th (one company)
2nd Brigade, Colonel Robert Burne:
1/36th
Portuguese Brigade, Brigadier General Frederick Eben:
8th Portuguese Line (2 battalions), 12th Portuguese Line (2 battalions)

7th Division: Major General John Houston
1st Brigade, Major General John Sontag:
2/51st, 1/85th, Chasseurs Britanniques, Brunswick Oels (eight companies)
Portuguese Brigade, Brigadier General John Milley Doyle:
7th Portuguese Line (2 battalions), 19th Portuguese Line (2 Battalions), 2nd Caçadores

Light Division: Brigadier General Robert Craufurd
1st Brigade, Lieutenant Colonel Sidney Beckwith:
1/43rd, 1/95th (4 companies), 2/95th (one company)
2nd Brigade, Lieutenant Colonel George Drummond:
1/52nd, 2/52nd, 1/95th (4 companies)
Portuguese Brigade:
1st and 3rd Caçadores

Ashworth's Independent Portuguese Brigade, Colonel Charles Ashworth:
6th Portuguese Line (2 battalions), 18th Portuguese Line (2 battalions), 6th Caçadores

Cavalry: Major General Stapleton Cotton
1st Cavalry Brigade, Major General John Slade:
1st Dragoons, 14th Light Dragoons

2nd Cavalry Brigade, Lieutenant Colonel Frederick von Arentschildt:
16th Light Dragoons, 1st Hussars KGL
Portuguese Cavalry Brigade, Brigadier General Barbaçena:
4th Portuguese Dragoons, 10th Portuguese Dragoons

Artillery: 48 guns

THE BATTLE OF ALBUERA

This order of battle only includes a small element of the Spanish army – Zayas's 4th Division that was heavily engaged alongside the British and Portuguese forces.

2nd Division: Major General William Stewart
1st Brigade, Lieutenant Colonel John Colborne:
1/3rd, 2/31st, 2/48th, 2/66th
2nd Brigade, Major General Daniel Hoghton :
29th, 1/48th, 1/57th
3rd Brigade, Lieutenant Alexander Abercrombie:
2/28th, 2/34th, 2/39th
Divisional light troops: 5/60th (3 companies)
Divisional artillery: 10 guns

4th Division: Major General Lowry Cole
1st Brigade, Brigadier General James Kemmis (absent on the day of the battle):
3/27th, 1/40th, 1/97th (only the Light companies of these three units were present on the day)
2nd Brigade, Lieutenant Colonel William J Myers:
1/7th, 2/7th, 1/23rd
3rd (Portuguese) Brigade, Brigadier General William Harvey:
11th Portuguese Line (2 battalions), 23rd Portuguese Line (2 battalions), Loyal Lusitanian Legion (1st battalion)
Divisional light troops: Brunswick Oels (1 company)
Divisional artillery: 5 guns

Portuguese Division: Lieutenant General John Hamilton
1st Brigade, Brigadier General Archibald Campbell:
4th Portuguese Line (2 battalions), 10th Portuguese Line (2 battalions)
2nd Brigade, Brigadier General Luiz Fonseca:
2nd Portuguese Line (2 battalions), 14th Portuguese Line (2 battalions)
Divisional artillery: 10 guns

Independent Brigades:
1st Independent Brigade (KGL), Major General Charles Alten:
1st Light Battalion (KGL), 2nd Light Battalion (KGL)
2nd Independent Brigade (Portuguese), Brigadier General Richard Collins:
5th Portuguese Line Regiment (2 battalions), 5th Caçadores (1 battalion)

Cavalry Division: Major General William Lumley
Heavy Brigade, Colonel George de Grey:
3rd Dragoons, 4th Dragoons
Portuguese Cavalry Brigade, Colonel Loftus William Otway:
1st Portuguese Dragoons, 5th Portuguese Dragoons (1 squadron), 7th Portuguese Dragoons, 8th Portuguese Dragoons (1 squadron)
Unbrigaded:
13th Light Dragoons
Divisional artillery: 4 guns

Spanish 4th Division: General Jose Zayas
1st Brigade, Brigadier General Cruz-Murgeon:
2nd Reales Guardias Españolas, 4th Reales Guardias Españolas, Irlanda Regiment, Voluntarios de la patria
2nd Brigade, Brigadier General Ramon Polo:
Imperiales de Toledo, Legion de Estranjeros, Ciudad Rodrigo Regiment, Reales Guardias Walonas, Zapadores

APPENDIX TWO: THE REDCOATS – ORGANISATION AND TACTICS

SCUM OF THE EARTH? – THE MEN IN REDCOATS

The men who donned the scarlet jacket of the British army were a fascinating and complicated group of men. Marshal Soult said of them after the Battle of Albuera: *'There is no beating these British soldiers. They were completely beaten, and the day was mine, but they did not know it and would not run.'*

These men who *'would not run'* had joined the army for a plethora of reasons. Some were patriots – keen to fight the French – others were drunks and criminals with no other options. Many were simply escaping the boredom of life on a farm or in a factory, picked up by unscrupulous recruiting sergeants in the local public house.

After taking the *'King's shilling',* the recruit would be whisked before the local magistrate and give his name, trade, place, and date of birth. He would then swear that he was not already a member of the army, navy, or marines. He would formally choose if he wished to serve for seven years without a pension, or for life with the promise of a pension once he retired.

A large proportion of Wellington's best soldiers had transferred from the militia. The militia regiments were full-time home service battalions, and their men were often of excellent quality with high standards of drill and discipline. They were induced to transfer to regular regiments with the offer of a large cash bounty or simply for the honour and glory of serving their country and potentially building a successful career.

The pay of a private soldier was not good, even by the standard of the times. A shilling a day was half of that earned by an agricultural labourer, and only a quarter of the daily wage paid to a skilled textile worker. To make matters worse, the army also deducted money from the soldier's pay to cover food and other expenses, leaving them very little.

The officers had very little in common with their men. There were those real-life Richard Sharpe characters who came *'up from the ranks,'*[138] but it was a difficult transition and very few made successful careers after gaining a commission. Most army officers had purchased their commissions – they had bought their way into the army, sometimes at exorbitant prices. This practice limited who could become an officer and meant that the officer's mess was filled with the sons of wealthy businessmen and aristocrats. Gaining promotion also depended on how much money you had, as Charles Oman explains:

> Promotion in the British Army at this period was working in the most irregular and spasmodic fashion, there being two separate influences operating in diametrically opposite ways. The one was the purchase system, the other the frequent, but not by any means sufficiently frequent, promotion for merit and good service in the field. The practice at the Horse Guards was that casualties by deaths in action were filled up inside the regiment, without money passing, but that for all other vacancies the purchase system worked. When a lieutenant-colonelcy, majority, or captaincy was vacant, the senior in the next lower rank had a moral right to be offered the vacancy at the regulation price. But there were many cases in which more than the regulation could be got. The officer retiring handed over the affair to a 'commission broker', and bidding was invited. A poor officer at the head of those of his own rank could not afford to pay the often very heavy price, and might see three or four of his juniors buy their way over his head, while he vainly waited for a vacancy by death, by which he would obtain his step without having to pay cash.[139]

HOW WERE THE INFANTRY REGIMENTS ORGANISED?

The British army of the Napoleonic era was small compared to the French, Austrian and Russian forces. In 1809, the army's entire infantry contingent comprised three regiments of Foot Guards, 103 regiments of the line, eight West-India regiments, eight veteran battalions, ten battalions of the King's German Legion and ten more various foreign units.[140] Some regiments, including the Guards and the 60th Royal Americans, had multiple battalions, but many had only one. The total number of infantrymen at Britain's disposal was less than 200,000, and many of these soldiers were needed for service across Britain's growing empire.

A line infantry battalion comprised ten companies. Eight of these were known as 'centre' companies and two as 'flank' companies. The Grenadier Company, comprising the biggest and most impressive looking men, would take the position of honour on the right of the battalion. While the Light Company, which included the fittest and most intelligent soldiers, traditionally stood on the left. Companies were often further sub-divided into platoons of fifty men and sections of 25.

In theory, at full strength, a battalion would number 1,000 men and 35 officers. But the reality was that during the Peninsular, it was very rare for a battalion to muster anywhere near this number – in fact; it was common for a battalion to only field 500 men.

A Lieutenant Colonel commanded a battalion. On paper, there would also be two Majors, ten Captains (one commanding each company) and approximately 20 subalterns (Ensigns and lieutenants). As with all armies, non-commissioned officers were the backbone of the regiment. There was one Sergeant Major in each battalion – this man assisted the adjutant and would be a master of drill and every aspect of military discipline. Below the Sergeant Major were several Staff Sergeants with specialised roles, such as paying the men or looking after the battalion's weapons. Each company would normally have two sergeants and three corporals. These men handled the day to day running of the companies and much of the administration. A good NCO would be an experienced soldier who could read and write and knew how best to manage and motivate the men under him. Then, as now, it was an incredibly important position.

BRITISH INFANTRY TACTICS IN THE PENINSULAR

The British army in the Peninsular was a well-oiled fighting machine. Highly disciplined, well-drilled, and trained to fire their muskets quickly, the thin line of redcoats defeated the massed columns of the French time and again. But how did they do it?

Let me briefly explain the two infantry formations that are most mentioned in this book. First, there was the column formation. The column was the fastest way to manoeuvre troops across a battlefield without losing cohesion. These blocks of men, usually made up of battalions, could keep a tight formation and be thrown quickly into mass attacks. The weakness was that while the men were in a column, very few of them could fire their musket. Therefore, according to the military doctrine of the time, these columns were meant to rapidly deploy into line formation just before engaging with the enemy. This would allow the advancing unit to bring the maximum number of muskets to bear, before launching their final charge. Changing of formation was a complicated business, and the French, over-confident after years of victory, often used their columns as battering rams to smash through the enemy using elan and weight of numbers. This tactic had been successful for them across Europe, but against the disciplined redcoats of the Peninsular War, it failed repeatedly.

The redcoats favoured meeting the French while formed in a two-deep line. They would stand silently, the front-rank kneeling with the rear rank standing behind them. Technically, according to the official drill manual, the British, like the other European armies, were meant to form a three-deep line, but lack of men forced the British army to improvise and soon the two-deep line had become the norm.

A classic British tactic was to form the line on the reverse slope of a hill, fifty metres from the crest. This protected the men from French artillery and skirmishers. As the French column crested the hill, the redcoats would open fire – volleys rippling along the line. We must remember that the smooth-bore muskets of the time were very inaccurate, hence officers preferred the men to hold their fire until as late as possible. Simple mathematics meant a battalion formed in line could bring more firepower to bear than one formed in a dense column, in which most of the men were hemmed in and impotent. After firing one or two devastating volleys, the British infantry would charge, with fixed bayonets and force the French to retreat in disorder.

Another important infantry formation that is mentioned in this book is the *'Receive Cavalry Square.'* As we saw at the Battle of Albuera, an infantry unit caught in the open by enemy cavalry could be quickly outflanked and charged from all sides. The result could be terrible. To avoid this, an infantry battalion could form a hollow square – with four ranks of men on all four sides. Two ranks would kneel with two standing, this formed an almost impenetrable wall of bayonets that the attacking horses would not charge. As you may recall, the Light Division successfully formed multiple squares at the Battle of Fuentes de Oñoro and were still able to manoeuvre effectively across the battlefield.

Despite the success against cavalry, the square could become a death trap for the defenders if the enemy could deploy sufficient artillery and infantry to support the attacking horsemen.

In the next volume of my *Military History Geek's Guide to the Peninsular War,* I will give more detail on light infantry tactics, artillery, and engineering. For more information on the cavalry, see the relevant appendix (interview with Marcus Cribb).

APPENDIX THREE: GALLOPING AT EVERYTHING – BRITISH CAVALRY IN THE PENINSULAR (AN INTERVIEW WITH MARCUS CRIBB)

Wellington was famously critical of his cavalry in the Peninsular. He wrote they were guilty of *'galloping at everything'*– becoming over-excited and losing their discipline and cohesion. But is this a fair criticism and what strengths did the British cavalry have in the Peninsular?

Marcus Cribb is a friend of mine and a regular contributor to The Redcoat History Podcast. He was formally manager of Apsley House (Wellington's London residence) and is currently writing a book on the Second Battle of Porto. You can listen to his interview below on the Redcoat History Podcast and watch it on my YouTube channel. Marcus also serves in the British army reserves, in a Yeomanry cavalry regiment, so this subject is very close to his heart.

CHRISTIAN PARKINSON

Could you start by giving me a bit of a background to the British cavalry of the period? Give us a sense of how cavalry regiments were organised and what the different types of cavalry regiments were.

MARCUS CRIBB

There were different types which were all organised similarly to each other, but they were split into two main branches – heavy and light. And they've all got different names. For the heavy cavalry there was the Household Cavalry, or Dragoon Guards, and Dragoons. In the light cavalry, there were Light Dragoons and Hussars. Later, after Waterloo, there were also Lancers. These regiments were really meant to be used in different roles – reconnaissance for the light cavalry; hitting home and smashing the enemy for the heavy cavalry. This wasn't always the case though, especially under Wellington. He was forced to use all of his cavalry in multiple roles, as he never had enough of them. You can't just have 700 or 800 men of the light cavalry sat back waiting during a major engagement, and likewise you couldn't keep all your heavies only for a rare charge in battle.

The light cavalry were primarily armed with sabres, which are curved swords, and they are very much meant to be for running at people and slashing downwards. They wore hats rather than helmets, often with fantastic flamboyant uniforms. The heavy cavalry typically wore armoured helmets, and they carried a long, straight sword. Generally, in the heavy regiments were bigger men on bigger horses, as they were far more of a punching force.

They organised heavy and light regiments roughly the same. Cavalry regiments didn't have multiple battalions like an infantry regiment. The regiments were organised into troops. Troops are meant to be 100 men (by the time of the Peninsular War this had been reduced to 80) working together under a senior captain with two junior officers. They would have a couple of sergeants, a couple of corporals, and one trumpeter. You would have ten troops in a regiment, so, in theory, up to 1000 men with the additions of farriers, saddlers and uniform makers. You would also have veterinary surgeons attached. The College of Veterinary Science had only been established six years earlier. So, it's a really new thing to have a qualified vet and their assistants attached to every regiment. That's forward thinking.

Two troops would form a squadron, serving under the senior captain. Often regiments would only send between two to four squadrons overseas, meaning most cavalry regiments in the Peninsular War could only field 400-800 men. They would leave men back in Britain to manage the depot, find new recruits, and organise remounts. Finding fresh horses was one of the biggest logistical problems faced throughout the war.

CHRISTIAN PARKINSON

One battle that was fought near the beginning of the war was that at Sahagun (21st of December 1808) which I covered in volume one of my Peninsular War history. The great Peninsular War historian

124

Sir Charles Oman called that one of the greatest cavalry actions of the war. Having read about it, it seems that man for man, the British cavalry, were superior to the French. Is that true?

MARCUS CRIBB

It is hard to prove broad statements. Probably overall, the British army in the Peninsular, as a whole, was slightly better than the French, given their combat record. But the French cavalry force was much, much bigger – at least until about 1812 when they lost so many of their horses and their riders in the disastrous Russian campaign. So, they [the British and French cavalry] tended to be well matched. The French cavalry were usually better led. They tended to have better officers with more experience. One of the popular statements about the British cavalry of the time is that 'they would gallop at everything and then gallop back again.' They have this reputation for overreaching. They'd go into an attack and then they would just keep going and keep going. This was famously exposed at Waterloo. At Sahagun, the difference is that Lieutenant General Lord Paget commanded the British – 'Handsome' Henry Uxbridge, as he became. He's a fantastic cavalry commander. He really knows how to use his soldiers and also how to use the ground to best effect. A bit like how Wellington could read ground for deployment, knowing how to use a reverse slope or go on the attack at the right time, Uxbridge [Paget] knows how to use the terrain, get around behind the French and attack them at the opportune moments. At Sahagun, he surprises the French so successfully that they are actually stationary when the British charge. They tried to defend themselves from a stationary position against a charging enemy force, which is really difficult to do. It was a stunning charge, catching the French off guard in the snow and cold of Spain in winter.

CHRISTIAN PARKINSON

Yes, I understand it was never a successful tactic during the Napoleonic era for cavalry to stand still while being charged.

MARCUS CRIBB

That's right. It's all about kinetic energy. It's about two forces of horse and man coming together, quick sweeps of the swords before passing and wheeling around. If you are stationary, your charging enemy has got the entire advantage. It's a bit like sailing, they've got the wind on their side, and they're coming in. That's why it worked really well.

The British cavalry began the Peninsular quite strong. They were coming out of a period of training, and they had gone through a series of reforms. They're very competent, but they were generally suffering from poor leadership. Any unit is only as good as its leaders. Uxbridge was replaced by Major General Charles Stewart – an interesting man, but not a fantastic cavalry commander. Sometimes he failed to charge at the right moment. During one action, his own cavalry officers could see that he was making the wrong decisions – sending them against a much larger number of the enemy, but he was unwilling to listen to their concerns. They really suffered under his leadership. Uxbridge [Paget] who, as we mentioned, was there during the Corunna campaign, is fantastic but ends up going back to Britain because he elopes with Wellington's brother's wife. It was an enormous scandal in Georgian society.

CHRISTIAN PARKINSON

Can you tell me a bit more about those cavalry reforms that the British army had gone through prior to the Peninsular War?

MARCUS CRIBB

The cavalry was a very fashionable arm to go into. For example, the officers were paying a lot more to gain their commissions than those in infantry regiments. But the cavalry hadn't been used very well in the conflicts before the Peninsular. Many units had been kept in Britain and Ireland, being used as a type of police force. They suffered because each regiment had its own de-centralised training and its own equipment – often dictated by the Regimental Colonel. So, there were some regiments that were found, for example, to have really weak swords, that shattered when hitting an enemy's. This was because they were buying low-quality blades at low prices. Other regiments would have really expensive uniforms. The lack of a coherent system was making them a less effective fighting force.

It was also observed that when they were fighting in the Low Countries, alongside the Austrians, the men were lopping so wildly in combat that they looked like woodsmen. Sometimes they would even cut off their own horse's ears. And so, John Le Marchant, a Brigade-Major who later became a Major General, observed this poor technique and wrote his ideas for a series of reforms and sent them to Horse Guards [British Army Headquarters]. He told them that the cavalry needed some standardised training and weaponry. Eventually, his thoughts were turned into a book which was adopted by the War Office – *The Rules and Regulations of the Sword Exercise of the Cavalry (1796)*. The book includes drills that the men would practice for hours; it also included the formations that all men must know and understand. Famously, there was also a thing called '*six cuts*,' which represented all the angles of cuts that the men would need to learn and drill. It was all about wrist and forearm strength. The book also came with guards, overhead positions, and also obviously sweeping down. And so everybody could practice this – the illustrations were meant to be drawn or pasted on a wall in the barracks. The other thing that Le Marchant did is he proposed the design of two main swords – a heavy cavalry sword, and the light cavalry sabre. These new designs were effectively a lot stronger than previous types. They had a real purpose.

The heavy cavalry sword had a wide hilt and basket, and it was really long so that it could be held out and used like a lance. They made it never to fail and it was incredibly strong. It had two tangs. You could hook it around the enemy's sword and disarm them.

There was also the light cavalry sabre. [at this point Marcus pulls a fine and well-maintained example of a cavalry sabre out from behind his sofa] The light cavalry sabre – 1796 pattern, was designed so that if you're on a horse, you're naturally going to bring this down with huge speed. It's got just a slight curve, so you can't hold it in a straight line and stab it into the opponent. What it's designed for is to bring that weight down upon the enemy. It was so effective that the French complained about it because they couldn't sew up wounds made by it. It was so powerful that the blade would go through both flesh and bone. The weighted blade had a huge amount of force behind it. Most importantly, it was then standardised so that all the light cavalry would carry the same swords; and all the heavy cavalry would have the 1796 pattern heavy cavalry sword. The only exceptions were that the officers tended to buy their own – but they would generally be a version of the standard issue, but with a nicer handle or a nicer grip.

CHRISTIAN PARKINSON

You presumably have practised with these swords; how do they feel?

MARCUS CRIBB

They feel like a really excellent weapon for what they're meant to be used for. There's a kind of stereotype about British archers during the Battle of Agincourt having huge right arms, and it feels like cavalrymen must have been the same. You really need to practice for four to six hours a day, which is what the troopers were doing – something we just don't have the luxury to do these days. It feels like these guys must have been riding around with a right arm twice the size of their left – I don't know if they've ever found any archaeological evidence of this, but I know of English Bowmen on the Mary Rose wreck whose bodies were found with enlarged right arm bones from similar exercises. They sometimes gave infantry and artillery officers these swords and you can understand why they would really struggle to use them, as these swords were designed to be brought down from a height. It's quite long, with a thicker end, and it would be quite difficult to use at ground level.

CHRISTIAN PARKINSON

Bernard Cornwell's Richard Sharpe famously carried a heavy cavalry sword. Is that completely unrealistic?

MARCUS CRIBB

That's right. In the books they refer to it as a *'butcher's blade.'* Sharpe carries the 1796 heavy cavalry pattern sword. I actually own one of the swords Sean Bean's character, Richard Sharpe, used in most of the episodes. It is a long blade, so basically the sabre edge would drag along the ground. It would need to be strapped very high on the waist. It would jangle around, not exactly practical if he's going to be running around rocks and skirmishing with his Riflemen. In reality, He would have been issued with a thin, slightly curved sword, which had been redesigned for the flank companies i.e., skirmishers – because they found that these light troops were far more likely to be engaging with the French in hand-to-hand combat. I have used one of these swords too and can say it is far better for quick action as well as lighter for all of his long range missions. But the heavy cavalry sword would be very difficult to wield from the ground. It would sometimes need a two-handed motion. Sharpe is meant to be quite strong, but he's not going to have the luxury of what a heavy cavalry trooper is doing, which is the six hours training with it every day. So, he would be at a genuine disadvantage. But, I think there's also that fear factor, i.e., if you've got some huge snarling guy coming at you with a massive sword, that would be quite intimidating. Muskets with bayonets fixed were effective, but they were basically a club with a pointy bit on the end. So, if a man wielding a sword could pass the bayonet, then he would have an advantage. In hand to hand fighting, the men would just be trying to punch, bite, and scratch the opponent to death. It could become very medieval.

CHRISTIAN PARKINSON

Yes, a very unpleasant form of warfare. Earlier you mentioned Le Marchant. Would his treatise be the cavalry equivalent of General Sir David Dundas' book *Principles of Military Movement*? Would that be a fair comparison?

MARCUS CRIBB

Exactly. He's the cavalry equivalent of Dundas. But Le Marchant is a relatively junior officer. I think he's a Major when he writes his book and then he gets promoted to Lieutenant Colonel. But they soon adopted his book as an official manual, which helps to streamline the cavalry and makes it a lot easier to train and organise. Obviously, officers can choose to ignore it, but they would be given a sword master and riding lessons too. It can be easily followed, and it's genuinely really helpful. It allowed commanders to know what to expect from their units, even those who are less experienced. When you get to the Battle of Waterloo, you've got regiments there that have not seen action in the Peninsular. Famously, there is the Scot's Greys and their glorious cavalry charge. These men hadn't fought in the Peninsular, but they were still perceived as good soldiers because they had received the same training as more experienced regiments. And that's something that you see today with modern armies.

CHRISTIAN PARKINSON

One reason, I read, that caused the British to have this reputation – for galloping at everything and losing their cohesion – was to do with the position of officers and NCOs in the ranks for a charge. In other words, they weren't hemming in the junior ranks as well as the French did. Therefore, officers lost control and the men went off and did their own thing, and it was hard to pull them back. Would that be a fair assessment?

MARCUS CRIBB

Relatively fair. On paper, there are meant to be sergeants to the rear and on the corners. Typically, the officers were meant to be out the front in a leadership role. While it's a broad sweeping stereotype, the officers tend to come from the aristocracy, and they want glory and honour, perhaps they want a nice little duelling scar – something they can tell the ladies about in the fashionable salons of London. Leading a glorious cavalry charge could be a fast route to celebrity.

As anyone who studies military history knows, war is 99% boredom, and the cavalry spend a lot of their time on picket duty, which is basically sentry duty and often very dull. But the cavalry were good at this. It was important work, keeping the army safe and gaining intelligence. Then, suddenly, when it comes time for a charge, you have all of this pent-up energy. At the Battle of Talavera, the 23rd Light Dragoons charged so hard that they didn't see a dry riverbed in front of them. Almost the entire regiment charged into it, with most of the horses breaking their legs. The survivors had to return to England with almost no horses. This mistake was purely about the leadership – the officers hadn't looked at the ground and they were keen to charge too soon.

CHRISTIAN PARKINSON

We've spoken extensively about the failures of the British cavalry (with the exception of the Battle of Sahagun). Can you give some other examples of times when the British cavalry during the Peninsular War performed well, and when Wellington was happy with them?

MARCUS CRIBB

Lots luckily. They were good overall at what they did. One of their most important roles was those picket jobs, that we mentioned earlier. They don't get many pages in the history books because they are often dull, but the work was incredibly important. The Allies would have their infantry pickets out, but beyond them you'd have your cavalry – often but not exclusively the light cavalry. They would create a screen at night-time to defend the forces and then the next day they would go off and do reconnaissance. And, as we know, Wellington's very reliant on his intelligence assets, he's got his exploring officers, he's got his local guerrillas and he's got his cavalry often going off and collecting intelligence and scouting towards the enemy, and it's something that they become very proficient at. The cavalry is going off very close to the French forces and skirmishing with them.

There were also the large set-piece battles. I believe Salamanca was Wellington's greatest victory, and it was there that cavalry played a crucial role. The Heavy Brigade, under Major General John Le Marchant, comes sweeping in on the French flank at the perfect moment. They had extended to the left, which is what Wellington spotted across the Spanish plain. They completely overrun the French positions, crashing through the front and second ranks, causing huge casualties. Unfortunately, during that charge, John Le Marchant was shot in the saddle and killed. So, we don't know how much of a fantastic cavalry commander he could have gone on to be. But the British cavalry caused such disarray, that Salamanca is a great example of just getting the timing right, pushing through the enemy but then realising when they've gone too far and coming back and supporting the infantry, rather than overstretching and losing complete cohesion.

CHRISTIAN PARKINSON

You mentioned recruitment earlier, and you talked about officers. I was also interested in the rank and file. Were they recruited the same way as the infantry? Did they have recruiting parties go around to pubs etc? Did the regiments differ on a socio-economic level from the infantry?

MARCUS CRIBB

I find it an interesting point that the cavalry actually wanted people who didn't have equine experience. They wanted all the recruits to be on an equal playing field. It's kind of the opposite of the First World War, for example, when they were forming the Tank Corps, they were looking for people with mechanical experience and relevant basic knowledge.

Despite the cavalry regiments wanting raw recruits who weren't already set in their ways around horses, they did seem to have more success recruiting in the countryside. Of course, Britain was still a rural nation in the 1800s and this gives the regiments an advantage – because it meant that many of the troopers had knowledge of horse welfare and could help to keep them healthy. We must remember that not only did the men love their horses, but they were also their weapon of war and they needed them. Besides the Veterinary Officer attached to each officer, each regiment had a Farrier Sergeant and a small cadre of farriers, who would have good equine care knowledge on top of their other role as blacksmiths.

The cavalry branch is not particularly more or less popular in terms of recruitment. I think overall, soldiers are joining the army at the time for a number of reasons including patriotism or adventure, but mostly for a wage and for food, or for a chance to escape Britain. So, the branch they join really doesn't matter that much as the wages are relatively similar.

Some regiments though did have specific recruiting areas. Often the colonels may have a grand idea of turning their regiment into a Scottish one, for example. But the reality was, like for many infantry regiments, that the best recruiting ground was often in Ireland and so a large proportion of the men would have been Irish. Even the 'English' regiments were often composed of around 30% Irishmen.

CHRISTIAN PARKINSON
What was Wellington's opinion of his cavalry in general? Did he try to avoid using his cavalry if he could?

MARCUS CRIBB
No, he definitely used cavalry when he could. He is often thought of as a defensive general, but he was definitely offensive when he needs to be. It is far more accurate to say he was a great all round tactician. He was an opportunist too, at Salamanca, he goes on the offensive and he certainly uses his cavalry. Like I said earlier, he doesn't really mind too much whether they're heavy or light regiments – at the end of the day, they're on a horse, they've got big sword and he was going to send them in. He would then leave the details to his cavalry commanders; he doesn't have a huge interest in

micro-managing them like he does with his infantry on the battlefield.

One of Wellington's regular complaints was that he didn't have enough cavalry. The constant scouting duties, as well as the general casualties in battle and disease meant that they were usually under strength. I think that he lacked time to really get to grips with his cavalry. He was so busy with the politics of Spain and Portugal, organising the exploring officers and the guerrillas. And he doesn't really like having a second in command – so he works incredibly long days. His focus was more on supplies and logistics.

CHRISTIAN PARKINSON

So, is it fair to say then that the cavalry's biggest impact on the Peninsular War was not its impressive charges in battle, but was more its less-glamorous picket duty and reconnaissance work?

MARCUS CRIBB

Yes, I think that is fair to say. During the course of the war, they make some really dynamic charges and that is what is most often written about, but the majority of their war was spent on picket duties and on scouting and reconnaissance missions. They are also doing duties such as protecting routes, providing rear-guards, and even assisting provost marshals with policing. So, a lot of their work was very mundane – but that is the reality of war. Wellington's army spends far more time marching than it does fighting. And so, although the cavalry may get accused of 'galloping at everything,' they actually performed most of their duties admirably.

APPENDIX FOUR: THE BATTLE OF ALBUERA, AN INTERVIEW WITH MARCUS BERESFORD, MARK THOMPSON, AND MARCUS CRIBB

The Battle of Albuera, fought on the 16th of May 1811, was the bloodiest fought during the entire Peninsular War. Other battles such as Talavera saw a larger total number of dead and wounded, but as a percentage of those engaged, the casualty figures at Albuera were shocking – one battalion losing 85% of its manpower with many others not far behind.

It is a battle full of drama and controversy: there were terrible mistakes; multiple colours were taken; entire battalions were virtually wiped out; reputations were made and lost.

This is a transcript of an episode of the Redcoat History Podcast – a conversation between myself and three experts on the Peninsular.

Marcus Beresford is a distant relative of Marshal William Carr Beresford, who commanded the Allied army on that fateful day. He is also the author of a book about his distinguished relative, and has written and researched extensively on the history of the Irish diaspora during the 18th and 19th centuries.

Dr Mark Thompson is an independent historian who has been researching the Peninsular War for forty years. He has written several books on the subject, including one about the Battle of Albuera.

Marcus Cribb, who we met in the previous Appendix, is currently researching and writing a book about Wellington's Porto campaign and the crossing of the Douro River in 1809. Until recently, he was the manager of Apsley house, Wellington's former residence in London. He is a friend of the Redcoat History Podcast and has been a guest on the show many times.

If you have already read the rest of this book, then you will recall that the British and Portuguese armies had spent much of 1810 on the defensive in Portugal. The incredible engineering feat known as the Lines of Torres Vedras had stopped the French invasion force under Marshal Andre Masséna from occupying Lisbon. Masséna's troops had been forced to withdraw to Santarem, and then eventually, in March 1811, ragged and starving, his army had retreated to Spain.

It was a brilliant strategic victory by the Allied commander, Wellington. But even as Masséna's army was on the run, the French were still a major threat elsewhere in the country.

Marshal Jean de Dieu Soult and his army had advanced from Seville in January and captured Badajoz in March. Wellington realised there was a need to split his army to face this threat. By rights and seniority, the commander of this force should have been General Rowland 'Daddy' Hill, but he was sick and had returned to England to recover his health. Wellington, therefore, turned to Marshal William Carr Beresford, the Anglo-Irish commander of the Portuguese army. Let's join the conversation...

MARCUS BERESFORD

It was made clear to Beresford that this was only ever a temporary command. This was pending Hill's return. Now, of course, by the time Masséna retreated from Santarem at the beginning of March [5th of March 1811], Hill still wasn't back in Portugal, and Beresford was therefore ordered by Wellington to take the 2nd and 4th Divisions and Hamilton's Portuguese Division south to relieve the siege of Badajoz. So that's the background.

MARCUS CRIBB

Beresford really needs to be given credit for his work in 1808-1810 where he reforms the Portuguese army. Beresford made them into a really effective fighting force. Initially the British were sceptical about their ability, but they proved themselves – very early on – to be able to stand shoulder to shoulder with the British veteran regiments and do an incredibly good job. I think that a lot of that credit was down to Beresford's admin command – his administration behind the scenes, which is not an interesting topic... but is really, really important when it comes to campaigning.

136

CHRISTIAN PARKINSON

Do you get the sense that there was a bit of reticence on Beresford's part to take up a field command? Did he prefer his job of helping the Portuguese to rebuild their army?

MARCUS BERESFORD

Well, I think he was fully committed to the rebuilding, but I think you've touched on a good point here – which is a desire for command. After the retreat from Corunna, when Beresford was back in England, he was offered the military command of Jamaica. He turned that down because he felt it would be a backwater, and he would not be involved in serious fighting. Likewise, when he was governor of Madeira, he was champing at the bit and wrote to Castlereagh repeatedly looking for a more active command.

MARK THOMPSON

There was actually another commander in between Hill falling sick and Beresford taking over. Initially the senior commander on the ground was William Stewart, who commanded the 2nd Division. This was in the very early days of January 1811. Within days Wellington was writing back to him, in response to his letters – and, I'm paraphrasing, comments like, *'Thank you for all your proposals on attacking the French – that is not what I asked you to do, and that is not why you're there.'* And this happened over three or four letters. By the end of the month, Stewart had changed his tune a little bit from wanting to attack everything in sight, to sending a bunch of letters where he was actually quite concerned that he didn't know what was going on, and was concerned that he wasn't in control. So, I think Beresford was seen very much as a stabilising influence. I think, quite rightly, that Wellington judged Stewart was not the right man for an independent command on the south bank of the Tagus.

CHRISTIAN PARKINSON

The fortress of Badajoz which Beresford and his troops were

now rushing to relieve should have been virtually impregnable. It had huge walls and a strong Spanish garrison, so what happened next?

MARK THOMPSON

When all this started in March of 1811, as Masséna was retreating, Badajoz was still in Spanish hands. Soult had started a siege at the end of January, and Wellington was desperate to get some forces down there to relieve it before Badajoz was lost to the French. So, when Beresford set off, he was going to relieve the fortress – it was only whilst he was travelling south that the message came up that the city had fallen. So, this was entirely unexpected. Wellington did not expect to lose the fortress and obviously the loss of it had a major impact.

Why this mattered was because Wellington's plan for 1811, when Masséna retreated, was to move north and retake the northern Portuguese border around Almeida and Ciudad Rodrigo. But that was done on the basis that he had full control of the southern entry points at Badajoz and Elvas. So, the loss of Badajoz completely messed up his strategy, and that's why the attempt was made to retake it immediately. Beresford was coming south with something around 15,000 troops – quite substantial, but not a big army. The numbers of French in the area were significantly less than that. As soon as Badajoz had fallen, Marshal Soult had returned towards Seville, because even in the few weeks that he'd been away he was getting worrying reports about the Spanish guerrillas and the Spanish armies creeping into the areas that were notionally under his control. So, Soult rapidly moved south and left several thousand Frenchmen in the area. They were outnumbered at that point. There was a very good chance that Soult would not come to the relief of Badajoz if the Allies tried to retake it. So, I think part of Wellington's thinking was that if Soult doesn't come north, we can retake Badajoz quickly and recover the southern entry point and continue with the main strategy. As we all know, that didn't happen, and Soult did come north again – and then we get into difficulties of resources around the siege of Badajoz. Initially it was Spanish held and then it was lost. I think Wellington was hoping that

Soult wouldn't come back – having decided that what he was doing at Seville was much more important than helping another French army.

CHRISTIAN PARKINSON

What were Wellington's instructions at this point? What did he want Beresford to do?

MARCUS BERESFORD

Well, in a nutshell. His instructions were: *Don't fight a battle unless you think you can win it.* Here was Beresford leading an Allied army which contained a very large Spanish element. Fourteen thousand Spaniards, 10,000 British which includes, of course, the King's German Legion and approximately 10,000 Portuguese – and this was the first time, the first battle in the Peninsular War, where all armies had fought under a unified command. At Talavera, we all know the difficulties because the Spanish were doing their own thing and Wellington had to suffer that.

CHRISTIAN PARKINSON

The Spanish army was notoriously badly led and had a terrible reputation amongst the British. Some of that was deserved, but much of it was unfair. For the siege of Badajoz and the subsequent battle of Albuera a number of Spanish generals with their respective contingents agreed to fight alongside the British and Portuguese. But who would be in overall command?

MARCUS BERESFORD

Beresford got on very well with Castaños. Castaños had a relatively small force – I think it was about 3,000 men. It wasn't the size of Blake's army – which was 8,000. Ballesteros weighed in with another few thousand to make up the Spanish 14,000. I suppose that what happened of course, when Wellington came down to inspect Badajoz and to look at a potential battle site at Albuera on the 20th of April, he gave Beresford very specific instructions, both regarding the siege of Badajoz and the fighting of the battle. And he said, *'don't start the siege of Badajoz until you've got a written undertaking from the Spaniards to do it as I want it done,'* and Beresford only got that written undertaking on the 8th of May – the day he started the siege.

There are other reasons why the siege was delayed. Wellington in ordering Beresford south did not anticipate that Beresford would have to conduct a siege and initially Beresford's force had no siege equipment. They had to get old guns from Elvas, some were 200 years old and split almost on first use. So, there were all those logistical problems as well. But Wellington gave Beresford very, very specific instructions. Just like he gave him instructions with regard to where to fight the battle should he have to do so. And with regard to the command of the battle – that was a very serious problem because, first of all, here were the Spaniard's weighing in with 14,000 men and why was a Spaniard not going to command this army? Secondly, Blake was a Captain General of the Spanish nation and had a claim to command, as did Castaños to lead these armies. Wellington had actually offered Castaños the command – but the Spaniard very magnanimous, said, *'no, I think Beresford should command,'* and that made life a lot easier for both Beresford and for Wellington.

MARK THOMPSON

Castaños gesture to say that the commander with the largest army should be in command was the thing that made it work. I wonder whether there was a sub text, not printed, where Wellington has said, *'If a Beresford doesn't get command, we ain't fighting,'* – because I can't think of an occasion where Wellington would have let a significant proportion of Anglo- Portuguese troops fight under a commander of which he had very little confidence. So, I just wonder whether there was something else going on that nobody's ever really talked about? But I don't think the battle would have happened if Blake had stood his ground – as for Castaños, I'm not sure. Wellington liked him, but liking is not necessarily the same as rating him as a general. General La Romana who died very unhelpfully in January 1811, Wellington said (and I'm paraphrasing here), *'he was a great guy and I got on really well with him, but he is useless as a commander.'* So, I just wonder about whether there's some other dynamics going on here i.e. that if Beresford wasn't given the command then the battle would not happen.

MARCUS CRIBB

At the time in the Peninsular War it was very difficult for the Anglo-Allied army to get enough manpower. Wellington was always saying he was short of things, especially artillery and cavalry, and basically, he could not afford the losses. Britain didn't have a conscription system like France did and could not replace men. And actually, just by fighting a battle, he just could not afford those losses if it wasn't going to be a victory. That's what he was really trying to avoid was any sort of decisive loss, where he just couldn't it back up, especially at this point where he's trying to fight a siege and manoeuvre/blocking campaign down to the south really split Wellington, whereas normally he did try to keep his force together. And that doesn't even count for [the siege of] Cadiz, which is a whole separate affair, mostly under General Graham.

CHRISTIAN PARKINSON

As is always the case in war, logistics were key. Badajoz was a tough nut to crack and Beresford's army did not have the firepower it required to break that hard shell.

MARK THOMPSON

Beresford was stuck with a problem, *'where can I find a siege train quickly to besiege Badajoz?'* Just putting a logistical context in place - for the siege of Ciudad Rodrigo in January 1812, they started planning to move the siege train in May 1811. It was six to seven months to move a siege train up. You cannot magic-up a siege train in a couple of weeks across the sort of terrain in the Iberian Peninsula. So, they effectively raided [the town of] Elvas, which was only about fifteen miles away. Many of the guns from there were very old.

The 10th of May was the day when Soult left Seville, heading for Badajoz. The actual operational part of the first siege of Badajoz was three days. You can't do anything in a siege in three days. They only got started sort of long enough to then have a much bigger job of taking everything away again. The thing that matters here is that nobody knew whether Marshal Soult would come back to relieve the city – and had he not come back, and you would have had weeks to work on the siege. It's a different ball game. Wellington's problem, as usual, was that he was trying to do them [sieges] against time. And so, if Soult hadn't come back, Badajoz would have fallen.

CHRISTIAN PARKINSON

As Marshal Soult marched his forces north to relieve Badajoz, Beresford had a big decision to make - should he fight? The decision he made was controversial, famously the great Peninsular War historian William Napier felt that it was a grave mistake.

MARCUS BERESFORD

When news of Soult's departure from Seville reached Beresford, I think on the 12th of May and [the news] was not only that he's left, but that he's advancing at speed, Beresford moved to have a meeting with the Spanish commanders. This took place at Valverde on the 15th of May. And Napier reserves his most intense criticism of Beresford for his decision to fight. It goes way beyond whatever he says about the conduct of the battle. He says that Beresford was right to raise the siege because otherwise he's going to be between a rock and a hard place when Soult came up to him. But Wellington, remember had said, *'If you've got the strength sufficient to fight a general action and maintain the siege, then fight.'* Now, Beresford was very uncertain and it's really clear this – Beresford was very uncertain about whether he should fight or not. And I think he was pre-disposed not to fight, but to retreat across the Guadiana River. The Guadiana River, for those who are not familiar with it, flows past Badajoz and just after Badajoz takes a very sharp right angle south and runs all the way down to the Atlantic Ocean. And Beresford had a *tete-du-pont* [a field fortification in front of a bridge] at Juromenha on the Guadiana, which he'd built, it was a trestle bridge. The original boat bridge had been swept away. We're talking about a time of year when the river was still in considerable flood. And he could use this bridge with *tete-du-pont* to retreat into Portugal. Now it was going to be difficult because getting a large army of 34,000 men across into Portugal was going to be a fighting retreat. But in a way the decision was taken out of his hands because when they discussed the tactics that they might employ, Blake had made it very clear that he wasn't going to retreat to Portugal and likewise, Benjamin D'Urban made it very clear that Beresford reckoned that Blake could never get back down the Guadiana, down to the relative safety of Cadiz again. So, Blake had put this gun to Beresford's head and essentially said, 'If you go back, I'm going to stand and fight.' And we know that Blake's force was 14,000 − coming up against them were either twenty-three or twenty-four thousand Frenchmen, including a very large and effective cavalry contingent. Blake was going to be wiped out. So, in a sense the decision was taken out of Beresford's hands. However, and this is really interesting, Napier flies a kite − more than a kite. He says that in fact Beresford's decision was forced on him by the British officers in his command − the officers of the 2nd and 4th Divisions who were really upset that they had not had a share of the glory at either the Battle of Bussaco or following Masséna on

his retreat into northern Portugal and Spain. They were itching for a fight, and they put serious pressure on Beresford.

MARK THOMPSON

I don't think Beresford had any choice and some of his letters, even before the battle and certainly after, were basically saying, '*this is not what I want to do I think we should be retreating. But with Blake having refused to retreat. I cannot politically, morally or ethically leave him to be destroyed.*' So, Beresford had no choice other than to fight the battle.

CHRISTIAN PARKINSON

And so, the decision was made to fight the battle. Why at

Albuera?

MARK THOMPSON

Well, I think the main reason why they decided to fight there was because Wellington said we are going to fight there. Wellington did say that the best place to fight a battle, if you choose to fight one, is Albuera. He specifically named it. If you look at it it's on the main Royal road, from Seville to Badajoz, it's on the main road. It's also in a central position, so that if the French tried to go to either east or west, there are lateral roads that Beresford could use. Almost every road in the area went through Albuera. So, there is a great sense that Albuera is the right place to fight the battle.

CHRISTIAN PARKINSON

Can you explain to us what the terrain was like around Albuera?

MARK THOMPSON

I think the most important thing to remember is that it was good cavalry country, that needs to be borne in mind when you look at the battle. In a more general sense, the battlefield was in the north-south plane. Albuera town was towards the left of the north-south area. There was a river running through Albuera – effectively running through the middle of the battlefield.

On the Allied side. It was very low rolling hills, so you could get a reverse slope, but you really are talking several feet – a very low sort of reverse slope. So, the classic Wellington features were there, but it was rolling hills, not big hills with drops on either side. However, on the French side, it was also rolling hills, not very high, but they were covered in woodland. There was some cover there, which, again, is an important feature on the battlefield. So, overall, if you stand on the ground to the north of Albuera where you can see the whole battlefield, most of it, even today, is still open. So, this was a very open area over which this battle was going to be fought.

The French advance guard had approached these hills

overlooking Albuera the night before the battle. The French had an opportunity to look at the potential battlefield. They could see some Allied troops, but not all of them. That's because some of them were on the reverse slope, but more importantly, a rather large chunk of them – such as all the Spanish – had not arrived at this point. Most of them didn't arrive till during the night or the early hours of the morning. So, Soult could see British troops in Albuera town. Soult could see British cavalry and some troops a number of kilometres to the south of Albuera. You get a reasonable idea of where the troops are going to be from what you can see, even if you can't see them all.

Soult had some good features as a general. He was actually very good at the strategy side, maybe not so much at the operational side, so his plan for the day was very good – a faint down the main road, which goes through Albuera itself, and then, using the cover of the trees, to do a long sweep to his left or the Allied right. And then come in along the ridge of hills straight on onto the Allied right. Soult's other argument was that he believed that the Spanish under Blake had not arrived and when they did – they would come from the south. If he swept round to the Allied right, he would place himself between the Anglo-Portuguese and the Spanish army. So, the actual overall plan for the battle was very good.

MARCUS BERESFORD

In terms of assembly of the two armies, Beresford had arranged with Blake that the Spanish army would be up in Albuera by midday – by twelve o'clock on the fifteenth [of May]. They didn't appear, and as Marcus said, they came in in dribs and drabs during the night. I think the main body probably only came in about two thirty or three o'clock on the morning of the 16th of May. Sunrise was shortly after four o'clock, about 4:20 a.m., and I find it almost inconceivable that Soult didn't realise the Spaniards were there. There was a hell of a commotion going on because the Spaniards didn't know where to go and assemble. Originally because the Spaniards weren't there, Beresford had had to put his cavalry on his right the previous day, as a precaution. So, he had to move those off and move the Spaniards in. So that was taking place in daylight, and they weren't even ready when the battle began. So, I just find Soult's claim that he was not aware the Spanish were there just fanciful.

MARCUS CRIBB

I agree. It seems very fanciful to think that he didn't see them, so it is very likely he was just dismissing them. I'm not quite sure of the motivations why. Because Soult was a very good tactician.

MARK THOMPSON

Soult claimed they weren't there in his report after the battle that he just lost. He was looking for reasons why it hadn't gone as he thought it should.

CHRISTIAN PARKINSON

The morning of Thursday, the 16th of May 1811 was dull and overcast. Now that the Spanish troops had arrived and taken up their allocated position on the right flank, the Allied army under Marshal Beresford was ready for battle. At approximately eight a.m. the French began their assault.

MARK THOMPSON

A French brigade under General Nicolas Godinot came down the main road and started attacking the town of Albuera followed by a heavy presence of French cavalry. So, everything at this point was going exactly as the Allied Army expected. Allied troops were starting to be moved towards Albuera town at the point when they started seeing the movement of French troops way off to the right – the Allied right. So, the overall plan up to this point, had gone exactly as expected, and bear in mind Soult's army was about 23,000 men, the vast majority of these ended up on the Allied right.

MARCUS BERESFORD

When it was reported to Beresford that the French were moving round with this left hook to come in on the Allied right he tried

146

to persuade, or he ordered Blake, to move part of his Spanish force round to face it. Blake was unwilling, he was unconvinced that this was the main attack. He thought this was just a feint. Beresford then went off to move the Portuguese division, I think slightly closer to Albuera. It was when he came back again that he realised Blake hadn't really done what he'd been asked to do or was being very slow about it. Eventually, of course, as we know General Zayas with the 4th Spanish Division did move round

to the right. He had the Real Guardias (Royal Guard) and, I'm very proud to say, the Regiment de Irlanda, and the Walloon Guards as well. And he moved round and faced the French onslaught with just his own division for a long time – and they fought very bravely, I think we must say that everybody agrees Zayas's troops fought very bravely.

Eventually, they were being overcome by sheer numbers. And then, of course, we arrive at this critical moment when Beresford ordered Stewart to move the 2nd Division forward and to get in line and to relieve the Spaniards who would presumably move back through the line. It's difficult for us to say, but I think Stewart undertook the task in a fairly ad hoc way. He started to move it, battalion by battalion, and it wasn't done properly. Colonel Colborne's brigade was over on the left and it traditionally should have been on the right of Stewart's division. He [Stewart] waited while Colborne brought his troops across. Colborne was very concerned about the manner in which they were advancing and made representations to Stewart, *'Can I pause? Can I get my men in the proper defensive order?'* And Stewart said, *'No, just keep going.'* I think the only explanation is either that Stewart was impulsive, or else he feared that the situation was so bad that he needed to get the troops into place.

MARK THOMPSON

Stewart was the general who initially took over from Rowland Hill – the one who spent the first couple of weeks of his command coming up with hare-brained ideas to attack the French. I don't think he had changed his spots over the coming months. I'm not a great fan of Stewart's behaviour on the day, I think it was close to irresponsible in open country. He knew that pretty much the whole of the French cavalry was in the area – visibility was appallingly poor both because of the weather and all the smoke in the area – and to move his whole brigade in line with no idea what's outside of it is . . .well history won't judge him well for what happened.

CHRISTIAN PARKINSON
So, what happened?

MARK THOMPSON
What happened is probably one of the biggest disasters to happen to the British Army, and certainly the biggest disaster in the Peninsular War.

We have set the scene quite nicely, we have a major fire fight going on between the French 5th Corps and, up to this point, Zayas's single division. Two thousand Spaniards were facing off against 8,000 Frenchmen. So, this was wonderful Spanish bravery. But Stewart's come up on the left-hand side of the French – so, he's coming around the right-hand of the Spaniards and is wrapping round onto the flank of the French in line; so that the front of his line would have been facing towards where the French were coming from. In these undulations in the hills though there was lurking a large number of French cavalry.

Latour Maubourg, the French cavalry commander, seeing Stewart's division, particularly Colborne's brigade, coming in, knew he had to do something to stop it. And he launched the nearest cavalry at it, which was the 600 troops of the Polish Vistula Legion – Lancers. This was a new breed of animal to the British troops. Along with them was the 2nd French Hussars, possibly the 10th Hussars as well – it gets a bit vague as to who actually took part in the charge. At this point the weather broke and they describe it as a hailstorm or certainly a thunderstorm. Visibility went to zero and several hundred French cavalry came down on the flank of Colborne's brigade and effectively they rolled it up. Infantry in line, hit from the side, particularly by Lancers, just cannot stand. The 1/3rd [Regiment of Foot], then the 48th and 66th were effectively destroyed in a matter of minutes by this brilliant French charge.

Again, maybe Stewart could have done this a different way. Colborne had certainly asked to protect his flank and been told that he couldn't. We must remember at this point that Colborne had been commander of the Brigade for probably a whole three hours – maybe only two by the time this event happened – because the brigade commander was actually William Lumley, who'd just been taken off to take command the British cavalry. So, Colborne's first experience of command was not pleasant.

CHRISTIAN PARKINSON
Marcus, can you just tell us what was special about Lancers? What were they?

MARCUS CRIBB
Oh, yes. This situation was really unusual, especially as the reports afterwards are quite horrific. The Lancers were typically Polish regiments, though at this point Napoleon's armies were actually recruiting from quite a wide part of Europe for lancers. Lancers have got a pole arm, so it gives them a lot more reach – almost like a knight jousting. British light cavalry and heavy cavalry will actually hold their sword out like a lance, but it's not going to have that the length that a spear would. The British see this famously at Waterloo and adapt some of their Dragoon regiments from 1816 onwards into Lancers.

But one of the big problems here with Colborne's division is that the men don't get time to form proper squares. So, they form what would be called a rally square, which is basically a huddle. Everybody huddles and forms a scrum that faces out with their bayonets fitted. It does give them some protection but because it's not a proper square, which is four ranks – two kneeling, two standing, they don't have that protection of the distance. So, when you are in a huddle everyone's standing, or maybe just a few are kneeling. So, it means lancers can get into that rally and stab.

MARCUS BERESFORD

There are several paintings of this both by British artists and by French artists. The lancers got right in close to Beresford and his staff. There is a painting of a lancer approaching Beresford, and Beresford unhorsing him. One of the things Beresford had was massive physical strength, and he reputedly unhorsed this lancer himself and then the lancer had the temerity to get up and try and stick him with his lance! Whereupon he was dispatched by one of Beresford's ADC's.

CHRISTIAN PARKINSON

Colborne's Brigade, including the Buffs [1/3rd] bore the brunt of this devastating cavalry charge. Casualties were horrific. The Buffs were almost completely wiped out and a number of colours were also captured - a disgrace for any regiment. But over the years, there has been some debate over exactly how many were captured by the French.

MARK THOMPSON

The loss of the colours of the regiment is an emotional and military disaster for that particular unit. But at some points in the battle the three regiments that were destroyed had their colours in enemy hands. So, this was the worst loss in any battle in the Peninsular War. I believe that four standards were taken – these were the colours of the 2/48th and 2/66th. They were the second and third regiments to be overwhelmed by the cavalry attack.

The colours of the Buffs are where the confusion comes in. It's confusing because at one point in the battle they had lost one of their colours. Their regimental colour was taken and was found later in the day by a soldier, an NCO in one of the Fusilier regiments. How it could get mislaid on the battlefield is somewhat bemusing.

The other colour is where you get the classic tale about Matthew Latham, who defended the colour. Not quite with his life –

150

he lost half an arm, [and] half his face. In one of the lulls in the cavalry attacks, he ripped the flag, the standard, off the flagpole and shoved it in his tunic. That's what was found on his severely injured body at the end of the battle. So, this is where the confusion comes around the Buff's standards. I think – possibly – where the confusion comes from is to do with whether you look at it from a British perspective or a French perspective. In a British regiment, the colours are the flags (I know... I'm not supposed to use that word), but it's that bit of silk and cloth which is the colour of the regiment. It is stuck onto a bit of wood, which they carry round. In the French army, the standard of the unit is the eagle. That's the big brass thing on top of the wooden pole. The bit of cloth that's flying around is not the important bit of your regiment. It's the eagle. So, there's two different military perspectives here. To the British, the cloth is the important bit, to the French it's the poll and what's on top of it is what is important.

Now, the French claimed they had taken the standards of the Buffs. But they're talking about the flagpole, the fitting on the top of the flagpole and some fragments of cloth attached to the standard. That's kind of my take, that the French took four pieces of cloth which were the standards of the 48th and 66th – and at some point, the French had the flagpoles and some fragments of cloth from the Buffs. That's my perspective. I'm happy to be challenged on it, but I think that's partially where some of the confusion comes from – your perspective of what the heart and soul of the regiment actually is.

After Colborne's brigade was destroyed the remainder of Stewart's division did come forward and continue the fire fight against the French 5th Corps – which is still standing at the bottom of the hill and has been by this point for more than an hour. Why 8,500 Frenchmen would stand at the bottom of a hill when there's less troops shooting at them from the top of the hill is just really difficult to fathom. This firefight continued and Beresford is in the area watching all of this. The remainder of the 2nd Division is now literally being demolished in front of his eyes and something needs to happen, otherwise the French are going to gain the heights and potentially start rolling up the army.

MARCUS BERESFORD

It's clouded with a bit of mystery, but this is probably the moment at which Beresford urged other Spanish regiments to get into the battle and they wouldn't. And I think it's felt that these were the regiments that had suffered so horrendously at the battle of Gebora against Soult on the 19th of February. They were somewhat unwilling to fight at this stage. It seems, and I am not condoning it, that Beresford himself then went off in search of Hamilton's

Portuguese division. Why he went off himself I don't know, but he was certainly trying to get Hamilton's division to move across from the left further to the right.

CHRISTIAN PARKINSON

With Beresford temporarily unavailable, searching for the Portuguese, the right flank of the army was leaderless. The only fresh British division close at hand was Lieutenant General (local rank) Cole's 4th Division, which had only arrived on the battlefield that morning from Badajoz. Despite their proximity to the heavy fighting Beresford had not wanted to use them – Not yet at least.

MARK THOMPSON

Cole was told not to move unless commanded to do so by Beresford and I think that's the key. Cole was covering between two high points, which covered the roads to Badajoz and the road to Valverde, which effectively was the road of retreat. That was the road that went to Juromenha, where the Allied bridge was across the Guadiana. So, if Beresford had to retreat that was the only way he could go. That's why it was so important to Beresford that that area was covered. So, I think that's key to explain why Beresford was looking for anybody other than the 4th Division to come and support the right flank.

CHRISTIAN PARKINSON

But, with the battle in danger of being lost twenty-five-year-old Lieutenant Colonel Henry Hardinge stepped up and decided to take matters into his own hands.

MARCUS BERESFORD

This was a subject of later dispute and letters, and not quite threats of legal proceedings. But it went for a couple of rounds at least because Hardinge, who was on Beresford's staff went up to Cole and allegedly persuaded Cole to move the 4th division down – to come around on the French left. Rooke, who was a Colonel, also was with Hardinge and supported Hardinge that this is what had happened. Cole maintained he took the decision. I don't think it matters very much because I think Cole saved the day by moving down in the way he did in echelon formation. And the way they dealt with both the French cavalry and later, the French infantry, saved the day.

MARK THOMPSON

I think the thing about Cole is that from where he was based, he had some visibility.–Throughout the battle there were constant comments from British soldiers and officers that they could see almost nothing because of the weather and the smoke; [and] because it was such a wet, rainy day. There was low cloud. The smoke had nowhere to go, so visibility was incredibly poor.

But at this point in the battle, Cole certainly had some evidence of what was going on off to his right, where Stewart was. He'd had remnants of Colborne's brigade come back to him – trying to escape the cavalry – so, he was fully aware of the disaster that happened to Colborne's brigade. I think there's absolutely no doubt that Cole was itching to come forward, [in fact] most of his staff were also itching for the division to move forward; and I think, looking at the whole situation, the right decision was made. They could not afford to wait because the right flank of the Allied army was close to collapse and waiting could have ended in defeat.

Where was Beresford at this time? I would also like to say, 'where was Blake?' I would also ask, 'where was Soult?' At this point in the battle, they all seemed to be fairly invisible. Now, the story that's generally accepted was when Beresford couldn't get the Spaniards to move, he wanted to bring Hamilton's Division forward – and for reasons that are lost in history Beresford went himself. The general observation seems to be that he had no staff officers left, so Beresford went himself.

But then as Marcus Beresford has just said, we now have Hardinge and Rooke, who are two members of Beresford's staff, wandering across to the 4th Division to talk about it. So, something doesn't quite add up in this story, but I think Beresford was looking for troops to come forward. I think it was absolutely the right thing to do. Whether Beresford and Hardinge and Rooke weren't together – [it appears] that they'd independently gone on different routes to try and look for a solution is the only thing I can think of. But Cole, without a doubt, he was the leader – he made the decision to move his troops, and the way he did it was absolutely masterful. He did talk with Lumley – the commander of the Allied cavalry – before he made the move. The Allied cavalry was much inferior in numbers and quality to the French who were right in front of them. Cole advanced with his Fusilier Brigade on his left with a column on the left-hand end for protection against cavalry. The Portuguese Brigade advanced on his right, which eventually became echeloned as they moved forward. On the right of the Portuguese was a group of Light companies in column to protect that right hand end of the line. So, this is probably what Stewart should have done earlier in the day. The French cavalry made a number of attacks on Cole as they advanced, particularly on the Portuguese, believing that the Portuguese wouldn't stand.

The French discovered that Portuguese advancing in line; and when they [the Portuguese] fire is an unpleasant experience, and having tried to charge them a couple of times, the French actually moved off and did not try another attack. So, this was a well-executed plan. Soult was clearly somewhere in the area because he could see this happening. The reserve for the French attack, on the right, was Werle's Division who were behind the 5th Corps. They were diverted to deflect Cole's advance and we got the third major fire fight of the day, between Werle's Division and the Fusilier Brigade.

154

CHRISTIAN PARKINSON

It was now that the battle became a brutal firefight, fought at close range with an intensity rarely seen during the Napoleonic era. Sergeant John Spencer Cooper of the 7th Royal Fusiliers later recalled, *'Under the tremendous fire of the enemy our thin line staggers and men are knocked about like skittles, but not a step backward is taken. Here our colonel and all the field officers of the brigade fell killed or wounded, but no confusion ensued. The orders were "close up" "close in" "Fire away" "Forward". This is done. We are close to the enemy's columns; they break and rush down the other side of the hill in the greatest mob like confusion. In a minute or two our nine pounders and light infantry gain the summit and join in sending a shower of iron and lead into the broken mass. We followed down the slope firing and huzzaring until recalled by the bugle.'*

MARK THOMPSON

This was a fire fight like no other, mainly because firefights tended not to last long because one side gave way. At Albuera both armies stood for hours, literally, at short-range pouring volleys into each other and that's what I think makes Albuera stand out from many other battles. We have to remember it's early afternoon by this point, and this has been going on since around nine or ten o'clock in the morning. Initially, the Spaniards against the French 5th Corps who stood for well over an hour, then came Stewart's Division. After the destruction of Colborne's Brigade, the other two brigades of the 2nd Division continued this fire fight against the numerically superior French who were standing below them in the cornfields. And then, the third attack comes in with the Fusilier Brigade coming forward and instigating another massive firefight.

CHRISTIAN PARKINSON

Normally, of course, the British would form line, fire one, maybe two volleys and then charge with the bayonet. What made them just stand there and keep swapping volley after volley with the

French on this occasion?

MARK THOMPSON

I think if you look at the numbers – the 5th Corps was about 8,500 strong, the Spanish initially (the Zayas Division) was about 2,000, the remainder of Stewart's Division was less than 2,000. Would you want to charge downhill into a mass of rather upset Frenchman, who outnumber you three or four or five to one, when there's 3,000 French cavalry loitering round as well?

CHRISTIAN PARKINSON

At this point in the battle with the Allied right involved in a desperate firefight, what was happening in the other sectors? Was the entire Allied line so heavily engaged?

MARCUS BERESFORD

There's not much happening on the left of the Allied position and the number of casualties suffered by Hamilton's men tells its own story – they had very little engagement. There was some artillery fire going to-and-fro across the river, but that's about it. Of course, in the centre we've got the King's German Legion desperately defending the village because that attack was being pressed forward. It may have only been a feint, but it was being pressed forward well.

CHRISTIAN PARKINSON

At this point then the KGL are quite heavily engaged in the village, the left flank is not too heavy, Cole's in this horrific firefight over on the British right flank, so what happens next? What's the next major development in the battle?

MARK THOMPSON

I think by this time you're getting towards the end of the battle – really the French, primarily the 5th Corps, who had stood taking close range musketry fire for a number of hours start wavering. Really at this point, the French had just had enough – quite understandably.

We now have Hardinge coming in again with his Superman cape, and then boldly ordering everybody senior to him around to attack the French and charge. Whatever the rights of this is, at this point the British advanced and the French, after hours of bombardment, gave way.

So, this was one of the critical points in the battle – the 5th Corps were effectively all the French infantry. So, when they gave way, apart from a tiny reserve, the French army had given way on the battlefield. But there were other things going on at this point.

MARCUS BERESFORD

The fact that the French had a superiority in cavalry enabled the cavalry to cover the French retreat and the Allies may have been too exhausted to follow anyhow. But the French cavalry maintained its discipline, its formation and covered Soult's retreat effectively.

MARK THOMPSON

A second Allied attack would have been exceedingly costly. It would have had to have been done by Spanish or Portuguese troops – which was a risk, because they were not battle hardened the same way that a lot of the British troops were. But Beresford and, I think quite rightly, just wouldn't have it. He wanted to stay where he was, consolidate his position on the battlefield and let the French decide what was going to happen next.

CHRISTIAN PARKINSON

And so, the Battle of Albuera – a horrific slogging match of a battle – slowly fizzled out with both sides battered and exhausted. The British had held their ground, but had it been a victory?

MARCUS BERESFORD

Yes, I think so. I think the Allies won. Soult had to retreat down back down to Seville. His army was seriously mauled, and he had failed to raise the siege of Badajoz. In fact, Beresford was able to send back the unused Portuguese division to resume the siege the very

157

next day. So, I think you can claim it as victory, and I think you need to see Albuera in context with the Battle of Fuentes De Oñoro. And the fact is that – although it was not immediately clear – after these two battles the French had been driven out of Portugal. And apart from one small incursion in 1812, they weren't to return. So, the theatre had moved from defending Lisbon to the Portuguese frontier and enabled Wellington to jump off into Spain in 1812.

CHRISTIAN PARKINSON

So, it was a victory, but one won at a terrible cost. Had it been worth it? The casualty figures were horrific.

MARK THOMPSON

The Allied casualties on the day were about 6,000. The French anywhere, typically between 6-8,000 or anything up to 9,000 depending on who you read. Soult's first reports said 2,800, which was a lie. I've picked a few of the battles out at random: at Salamanca, there was 5,500 casualties so that was less [than Albuera]. Talavera saw seven and a half thousand – so that was more. The Siege of Badajoz, in 1812, was just shy of 5,000 Allied casualties. But the three that I've just mentioned, as a percentage of the army, Salamanca was about 10%, Talavera was about 15% – although the British proportion of that was nearer thirty which is pretty horrendous.

Badajoz was about 18% of the Allied army. The numbers move around a lot, but if you look at the 6,000 casualties at Albuera that was about seventeen percent of the army. If you start breaking that down, the bulk of those casualties were British. So, the casualties were 40%. The Spanish casualties were about 9%, the Portuguese about 4%. If we look at the 2nd Division, Colborne's Brigade, which was destroyed by the French, took 69% casualties across the brigade. The Buffs 85% casualties. The 2/48th *only* 76% casualties. The 66th suffered 62% casualties. Even the 2/31st, that did manage to form square, had 40% casualties. Hoghton's Brigade, which actually took part in the firefight after Coleborne's brigade was destroyed – 62% casualties in the brigade. Myers Brigade, the Fusilier Brigade, in the 4th Division took 52% casualties. So, the casualties in the British units were utterly horrendous.

But let's go back to the Spanish, Zayas took most of the casualties in the Spanish army during the battle. Their casualties were 30%, that would be considered catastrophic in any normal battle. So, I think that says more than anything else that Zayas's troops stood their ground and fought well throughout the battle. Were the French casualties any better? 5th Corps: 3,000 out of 8,500 men – that's 30-35% casualties. They stood for three to four hours

being shot at without a break. Even Werle, the reserve division on that side, suffered 25% casualties.

So, these are just horrendous numbers and that's why Albuera tends to get the title of the bloodiest battle [of the Peninsular]. It wasn't the biggest, but the proportion of casualties, particularly in the British units was incredibly high. There were literally entire battalions destroyed at Albuera, and some of them never fought again by themselves – and certainly through most of 1811, they fought in provisional battalions, where the remaining soldiers were grouped together with other battalions to form something like a workable force. So that's why Albuera always has the word 'bloody' attached to it.

MARCUS BERESFORD

Mark has hit it on the head. It is because of these horrific losses in the British regiments that it's highlighted for us. And when you think that the Buffs lost 85% of their strength at Albuera that's a really shocking number. No other regiment, I think, suffered quite that loss in any other Peninsular War battle. So, it really stands out.

CHRISTIAN PARKINSON

Beresford was particularly shaken by the day's fighting. It had been a slogging match like no other. Despite the Allied victory, things had not gone well. So, in the final analysis had Beresford performed well?

MARK THOMPSON

We seem to have got some disconnects going on here between Beresford and some of his staff. Bear in mind, Beresford's command is new, and his staff is new – they haven't learned to work together yet. And there's certainly some activity during the battle where Beresford and his staff seemed to be not quite on the same page: we've got the French flank attack which was brilliant strategy by Soult; we've got Blake refusing to move and the loss of the Spanish infantry who are unable to manoeuvre on the battle.

We didn't pick this up when we talked about Stewart advancing with the 2nd Division, but he wasn't given orders to attack – he decided to do that himself. So, Beresford has seen the 2nd Division attack without orders; we've then seen Beresford riding off to try and find Hamilton's division which wasn't where he left it because the first ADC he sent couldn't find it. Beresford's then gone off to find them, so he's down somewhere near Albuera. He turns around and Cole, who's got specific instructions not to move, is advancing into the right flank. So, you look at it from his perspective and he is not having a good day.

CHRISTIAN PARKINSON

Sounds like there's a bit of a command-and-control breakdown.

MARK THOMPSON

Yes, that's something I'm wondering. I think the issue here was that the visibility on the battlefield was so poor. How can you lose a division of 5,000 men? Now, I'm assuming then that these people were not incompetent; so, you have to assume that visibility was so poor that you just could not see where troops were – you had to literally ride round the battlefield to find people. You couldn't stand on the hill and say, '*oh, there they are we will ride down and give him an order,*' and I think that's what was happening throughout a lot of this battle. There was terrible visibility, and so people were feeling their way around the battlefield and that makes life difficult. And it also makes commanders very nervous.

MARCUS BERESFORD

I think. What is important is that Wellington stood by Beresford. Wellington said to Beresford, '*I have no doubt you have got the better of Soult and you should be justifiably proud of what has happened on the day.*' So, you know, Beresford was shocked, I reckon he had P.T.S.D. (Post Traumatic Stress Disorder) as a result of this. He was really shocked, and he was depressed for weeks afterwards.

MARK THOMPSON

I will stick my neck out and say, Soult lost Albuera rather than Beresford won Albuera. His [Soult's] advance to Albuera was brilliant his movements around the right flank of the Allies was brilliant. And then he went to sleep. Why would you leave 14,000 French troops at the bottom of a hill, facing a much smaller number of Allied troops and stand there in a firefight for four hours? Particularly when you've got a superiority in cavalry. I think it could have gone horribly wrong.

If Wellington was there, would it have been any different? The problems wouldn't have changed. I think Wellington brought to most battles, the same as what Napoleon brought to most battles – when he was there nobody argued with him about who was in command. So, Wellington might have made a difference, but he was still dealing with the same troops and the same problem. It might have been better, and Wellington might have ended the day with less casualties. He would still have won the day. So, the difference was that there might have been less casualties. The worst of the casualties at Albuera were caused by Stewart. Now, Stewart could still have done that stupid activity if Wellington was on the battlefield. So, I think that 'what ifs' are always a bit unhelpful. I don't think the overall result of the day would have changed materially if Wellington was there.

MARCUS BERESFORD

Wellington writes to Beresford, and it is very interesting. I have a quote here somewhere. '*You could not be successful in such an action without a large loss, and we must make up our minds to affairs of this kind sometimes or give up the game.'* What Wellington also says to his other generals, leading on into 1812-1813, *'some of you might be better generals, more talented strategists, but Beresford is the best man to ensure that the troops are fed and are there; and he'll get everything in order.'* He was effectively saying that Beresford was a wonderful administrator.

And in 1813, when the issue arises again, about who should take over if Wellington has to go to Catalonia – which was a distinct possibility in the autumn of 1813. He makes it very clear to the British government that it should be Beresford. And he has a battle on his hands with the Duke of York, in particular. In fact, I think Liverpool or Castlereagh – one of them supported Wellington. But he makes it very clear that – if Wellington is incapacitated for any reason, or if he has to go to Catalonia, or if he is wounded or whatever it is – Beresford should take over on a temporary basis. Now, whether they'd ever have allowed Beresford to take over on a temporary basis is another matter. But I just want to emphasise this as showing Wellington's view of Beresford. He had retained confidence in him.

CHRISTIAN PARKINSON
And so there you have it. Question mark remains over Beresford's performance at the battle, but he retained the support of Wellington and continued to prove himself to be a solid commander throughout the rest of the war. After the French withdrew from the battlefield of Albuera, Beresford returned to Badajoz to continue the siege. But despite the arrival of Wellington, it was quickly called off and the Allied army was forced to withdraw.

162

[1] Simmons, George. *A British Rifle Man, The Journals and Correspondence of Major George Simmons, Rifle Brigade, during the Peninsular War and the Campaign of Waterloo*, (A. & C. Black, 1899), p. 2.

[2] Napier, William, *History of the War in the Peninsular and in the South of France from the Year 1807 To the Year 1814, Volume Three*, (Reprint by Constable and Constable LTD, 1993), p. 291. Major M'Leod or McLeod as I've sometimes seen him referred to by other sources was killed in 1812 during the storming of Badajoz.

[3] Leach, Jonathan, *Rough Sketches of the Life of an Old Soldier*, (London, 1831), p. 150.

[4] Bart, Sir Richard George Augustus Levinge, *Historical Records of the Forty-Third Regiment, Monmouthshire Light Infantry*, (London, 1868), pp. 132-133.

[5] Wellington, the Duke of, K.G., *Supplementary Despatches, Correspondence, and Memoranda, of Field Marshal Arthur Duke of Wellington, K.G., Volume VI*, (London, 1860), p. 563.

[6] For the full story of the Battle of Talavera and the retreat from Spain you can read my previous book *The Military History Geeks Guide to...The Peninsular War, Volume One*.

[7] Bamford, Andrew, *The Guardiana Fever Epidemic*, (napoleon-series.org, read on the 30th of January, 2021).

[8] Cooper, John Spencer, *Rough Notes of Seven Campaigns in Portugal Spain France and America*, (Carlisle G and T Coward LTD, 1914), pp. 35-36.

[9] Schaumann, August, *On the Road with Wellington, Diary of a War Commissary*, (Reprint by Greenhill Books, 1999), p. 229.

[10] Oman, Charles, *A History of the Peninsular War, Volume Three*, (Clarendon Press, 1908), p. 209.

[11] Quoted in Bryant, Arthur. *The Years of Victory: 1802-1812*, (Endeavour Press, Kindle Edition).

[12] Simmons, George. *A British Rifle Man, The Journals and Correspondence of Major George Simmons, Rifle Brigade, during the Peninsular War and the Campaign of Waterloo*, (A. & C. Black, 1899), pp. 53-53.

[13] Lipscombe, Nick, *The Peninsular War Atlas*, (Osprey Publishing, 2014), p. 168.

[14] Oman, Charles, *A History of the Peninsular War, Volume Three*, (Clarendon Press, 1908), p. 273.

[15] Tomkinson, Lieutenant-Colonel William, *The Diary of a Cavalry Officer in the Peninsular and Waterloo Campaigns*, (Swann Sonnenschein and Co, 1894), p. 42.

[16] Even by the standards of the time Picton's behaviour while the governor of Trinidad was controversial. He had been involved with the slave trade and authorised the torture of a young mixed-race girl who had allegedly assisted her lover to burgle a house.

163

[17] Quoted in Bryant, Arthur, *The Years of Victory: 1802-1812,* (Endeavour Press, Kindle Edition).

[18] Sherer, Moyle, *Recollections of the Peninsular,* (London, 1823), pp. 107-108.

[19] Schaumann, August, *On the Road with Wellington, Diary of a War Commissary,* (Reprint by Greenhill Books, 1999), p.246.

[20] Grattan, William, *Adventures of the Connaught Rangers From 1808-1814,* (Henry Colburn, 1847), pp. 28-29.

[21] Weller, Jac. *Wellington in the Peninsula (Napoleonic Library),* (Frontline Books. Kindle Edition).

[22] Grattan, William, *Adventures of the Connaught Rangers From 1808-1814,* (Henry Colburn, 1847), p. 31.

[23] Ibid., p. 33.

[24] Ibid., p. 35.

[25] Leith-Hay, Sir Andrew, *A Narrative of the Peninsular War,* (London, 1829), p. 164.

[26] Oman, Charles, *A History of the Peninsular War, Volume Three,* (Clarendon Press, 1908), p. 377.

[27] Bart, Sir Richard George Augustus Levinge, *Historical Records of the Forty-Third Regiment, Monmouthshire Light Infantry,* (London, 1868), p. 136.

[28] Moorsom, W. S., *Historical Record of the Fifty-Second Regiment (Oxfordshire Light Infantry),* (London, 1860), p. 125.

[29] Maempel, Johann Christian, *Adventures of a Young Rifleman,* (London, 1826), p. 193.

[30] Weller, Jac, *Wellington in the Peninsula (Napoleonic Library),* (Frontline Books, Kindle Edition).

[31] Schaumann, August, *On the Road with Wellington, Diary of a War Commissary,* (Reprint by Greenhill Books, 1999), p. 254.

[32] Kincaid, Captain, *TALES FROM THE RIFLE BRIGADE: Adventures in the Rifle Brigade Random Shots from a Rifleman: "Adventures in the Rifle Brigade" AND "Random Shot",* (Pen and Sword, Kindle Edition).

[33] Leslie, Colonel Charles, *Military Journal of Colonel Leslie, K.H., of Balquhain,* (Aberdeen University Press, 1887), pp. 208-209.

[34] Schaumann, August, *On the Road with Wellington, Diary of a War Commissary,* (Reprint by Greenhill Books, 1999), p. 264.

[35] Many writers talk of there being three lines, but work on a fourth line was started in December 1810 which covered the south bank of the River Tagus.

[36] Robertson, Ian. *A Commanding Presence – Wellington in the Peninsular 1808-1814*. (Spellmount Limited, 2008), p. 173.

[37] Leslie, Colonel Charles, *Military Journal of Colonel Leslie, K.H., of Balquhain*, (Aberdeen University Press, 1887), p. 212.

[38] Leith-Hay, Sir Andrew, *A Narrative of the Peninsular War*, (London, 1829), p. 174.

[39] Anonymous (though it is actually Private Thomas Pococke), *Journal of a Soldier of the 71st or Glasgow Regiment Highland Light Infantry from 1806-1815*, (Edinburgh, 1819), pp. 115-117.

[40] Kincaid, Captain, *TALES FROM THE RIFLE BRIGADE: Adventures in the Rifle Brigade Random Shots from a Rifleman: "Adventures in the Rifle Brigade" AND "Random Shot"* , (Pen and Sword, Kindle Edition).

[41] Sherer, Moyle, *Recollections of the Peninsular*, (London, 1823), pp. 122-123.

[42] Cooper, John Spencer, *Rough Notes of Seven Campaigns in Portugal Spain France and America*, (Carlisle G and T Coward LTD, 1914), p. 51.

[43] Anonymous (though it is actually Private Thomas Pococke), *Journal of a Soldier of the 71st or Glasgow Regiment Highland Light Infantry from 1806-1815*, (Edinburgh, 1819), pp. 120-121.

[44] Wellington, the Duke of, K.G., *Supplementary Despatches, Correspondence, and Memoranda, of Field Marshal Arthur Duke of Wellington, K.G., Volume VI*, (London, 1860), p. 632.

[45] Quoted in Bryant, Arthur, *The Years of Victory: 1802-1812*, (Endeavour Press, Kindle Edition).

[46] Leach, Jonathan, *Rough Sketches of the Life of an Old Soldier*, (London, 1831), p. 178.

[47] Tomkinson, Lieutenant-Colonel William, *The Diary of a Cavalry Officer in the Peninsular and Waterloo Campaigns*, (Swann Sonnenschein and Co, 1894), p. 67.

[48] Schaumann, August, *On the Road with Wellington, Diary of a War Commissary*, (Reprint by Greenhill Books, 1999), p. 278.

[49] Kincaid, Captain, *TALES FROM THE RIFLE BRIGADE: Adventures in the Rifle Brigade Random Shots from a Rifleman: "Adventures in the Rifle Brigade" AND "Random Shot"*, (Pen and Sword, Kindle Edition).

[50] Lipscombe, Nick, *The Peninsular War Atlas*, (Osprey Publishing, 2014), p. 198

[51] Maempel, Johann Christian, *Adventures of a Young Rifleman*, (London, 1826), p. 195.

[52] Cooper, John Spencer, *Rough Notes of Seven Campaigns in Portugal Spain France and America*, (Carlisle G and T Coward LTD, 1914), p. 55.

[53] Leach, Jonathan, *Rough Sketches of the Life of an Old Soldier,* (London, 1831), p. 201.

[54] Schaumann, August, *On the Road with Wellington, Diary of a War Commissary*, (Reprint by Greenhill Books, 1999), p. 290.

55 Maempel, Johann Christian, *Adventures of a young Rifleman*, (London, 1826), p. 195.

56 Kincaid, Captain, *TALES FROM THE RIFLE BRIGADE: Adventures in the Rifle Brigade Random Shots from a Rifleman: "Adventures in the Rifle Brigade" AND "Random Shot"*, (Pen and Sword, Kindle Edition).

57 Schaumann, August, *On the Road with Wellington, Diary of a War Commissary*, (Reprint by Greenhill Books, 1999), pp. 290-291.

58 Erskine was temporarily in command of the Light Division during this period and showed himself to be grossly incompetent. Wellington told Horse Guards that Erskine was a 'madman.'

59 Kincaid, Captain, *TALES FROM THE RIFLE BRIGADE: Adventures in the Rifle Brigade Random Shots from a Rifleman: "Adventures in the Rifle Brigade" AND "Random Shot"*, (Pen and Sword, Kindle Edition).

60 Bart, Sir Richard George Augustus Levinge, *Historical Records of the Forty-Third Regiment, Monmouthshire Light Infantry*, (London, 1868), p. 145.

61 Moorsom, W. S., *Historical Record of the Fifty-Second Regiment (Oxfordshire Light Infantry)*, (London, 1860), p. 139.

62 Donaldson, Joseph, *Recollections of the Eventful Life of a Soldier*, (G.B. Zieber and Co, 1845), p. 116.

63 Surtees, William, *Twenty-Five Years in the Rifle Brigade*, (Edinburgh, 1833), pp. 108-109

64 Blakeney, Robert, *A Boy in the Peninsular*, (London, 1899), pp. 175-177.

65 Delavoye, Alex, *Life of Thomas Graham, Lord Lynedoch*, (London, 1880), pp. 463-464.

66 Surtees, William, *Twenty-Five Years in the Rifle Brigade*, (Edinburgh, 1833), pp. 111-112.

67 Delavoye, Alex, *Life of Thomas Graham, Lord Lynedoch*, (London, 1880), pp. 465-466.

68 Blakeney, Robert, *A Boy in the Peninsular*, (London, 1899), pp. 184-185.

69 Ibid., pp. 187-188.

70 Surtees, William, *Twenty-Five Years in the Rifle Brigade*, (Edinburgh, 1833), p. 118.

71 Blakeney, Robert, *A Boy in the Peninsular*, (London, 1899), p. 189.

72 Oman, Charles, *A History of the Peninsular War, Volume Four*, (Clarendon Press, 1911), p. 115.

73 Fraser, Edward, *The Soldiers Whom Wellington Led: Deeds of Daring, Chivalry, and Renown*, (London Methuen, 1913), pp. 137-138.

74 Patrick Masterson's descendent James Masterson became an officer in the Devonshire Regiment and won a Victoria Cross at the Siege of Ladysmith during the 2nd Anglo-Boer War.

[75] Cadell, Charles, *Narrative of the Campaigns of the Twenty-Eighth Regiment, Since Their Return from Egypt in 1802*, (London, 1835), pp. 95-96.

[76] Delavoye, Alex, *Life of Thomas Graham, Lord Lynedoch*, (London, 1880) p. 469.

[77] Surtees, William, *Twenty-Five Years in the Rifle Brigade*, (Edinburgh, 1833), pp. 122-123.

[78] Kincaid, Captain, *TALES FROM THE RIFLE BRIGADE: Adventures in the Rifle Brigade Random Shots from a Rifleman: "Adventures in the Rifle Brigade" AND "Random Shot"*, (Pen and Sword, Kindle Edition).

[79] Oman, Charles, *A History of the Peninsular War, Volume Four*, (Clarendon Press, 1911), p. 307.

[80] Donaldson, Joseph, *Recollections of the Eventful Life of a Soldier*, (G.B. Zieber and Co, 1845), p. 123.

[81] Ibid., pp. 124-125.

[82] Ibid., p. 125.

[83] Anonymous (though it is actually Private Thomas Pococke), *Journal of a Soldier of the 71st or Glasgow Regiment Highland Light Infantry from 1806-1815*, (Edinburgh, 1819), pp. 131-133.

[84] Ibid., pp. 134-135.

[85] Tomkinson, Lieutenant-Colonel William, *The Diary of a Cavalry Officer in the Peninsular and Waterloo Campaigns*, (Swann Sonnenschein and Co, 1894), pp. 100-101.

[86] Liddell Hart, B.H (Editor), *The Letters of Private Wheeler 1809-1828*, The Alden Press, 1998), pp. 54-55.

[87] Kincaid, Captain John, *Adventures in the Rifle brigade, in the Peninsula, France, and the Netherlands, from 1809 to 1815*, (London, 1830), p. 74.

[88] Liddell Hart, B.H (Editor), *The Letters of Private Wheeler 1809-1828*, (The Alden Press, 1998), p. 55.

[89] Napier, William, *History of the War in the Peninsular and in the South of France from the Year 1807 To the Year 1814, Volume Three*, (Reprint by Constable and Constable LTD, 1993), p .520.

[90] Anonymous (though it is actually Private Thomas Pococke), *Journal of a Soldier of the 71st or Glasgow Regiment Highland Light Infantry from 1806-1815*, (Edinburgh, 1819), pp. 136-137.

[91] Grattan, William, *Adventures of the Connaught Rangers From 1808-1814*, (Henry Colburn, 1847), p. 66.

[92] Ibid., p. 67.

[93] In this Grattan appears to be mistaken – it seems he mistook French Grenadiers in their bearskins for the Imperial Guard.

[94] Grattan, William, *Adventures of the Connaught Rangers From 1808-1814*, (Henry Colburn, 1847), pp. 67-69.

[95] Simmons, George, *A British Rifle Man, the Journals and Correspondence of Major George Simmons, Rifle Brigade, During the Peninsular War and the Campaign of Waterloo*, (A. & C. Black, 1899), p. 172.

[96] Oman, Charles, *A History of the Peninsular War, Volume Four*, (Clarendon Press, 1911), p. 335.

[97] Ibid., p. 341.

[98] This is a quote from a letter to his brother, dated 2nd July, 1811.

[99] I have seen different figures but this is the number that Oman cites.

[100] Jones, Sir John T., *Journal of The Sieges Carried on By the Army Under Wellington, Volume 1*, (John Weale, London, 1846), p. IX

[101] Oman, Charles, *A History of the Peninsular War, Volume Four*, (Clarendon Press, 1911), p. 276.

[102] Sherer, Moyle, *Recollections of the Peninsular*, (London, 1823), pp. 150-151.

[103] Ibid., pp. 151-152.

[104] Cooper, John Spencer, *Rough Notes of Seven Campaigns in Portugal Spain France and America*, (Carlisle G and T Coward LTD, 1914), p. 61.

[105] Boutflower, Charles, *The Journal of an Army Surgeon During the Peninsular War*, p. 90

[106] Wellington's dispatch, quoted in Oman, Charles, *A History of the Peninsular War, Volume Four*, (Clarendon Press, 1911), p. 280.

[107] Leslie, Colonel Charles, *Military Journal of Colonel Leslie, K.H., of Balquhain*, (Aberdeen University Press, 1887), p. 219.

[108] Ibid., pp. 219-220.

[109] Sherer, Moyle, *Recollections of the Peninsular*, (London, 1823), p. 159.

[110] Oman, Charles, *A Prisoner of Albuera*, Blackwood's Magazine (July-December, 1908), p. 427.

[111] Groves, Percy J, *The 66th Berkshire Regiment*, (Hamilton and Adams, 1887), p. 53.

[112] Oman, Charles, *A Prisoner of Albuera*, Blackwood's Magazine (July-December, 1908), p. 428.

[113] Oman, Charles, *A History of the Peninsular War, Volume Four*, (Clarendon Press, 1911), p. 386.

[114] Leslie, Colonel Charles, *Military Journal of Colonel Leslie, K.H., of Balquhain*, (Aberdeen University Press, 1887), p. 222.

[115] Sherer, Moyle, *Recollections of the Peninsular*, (London, 1823), p. 161.

[116] Warre, H.J, *Historical Records of the 57th or West Middlesex Regiment of Foot*, (London, 1878), p. 53.

[117] Cooper, John Spencer, *Rough Notes of Seven Campaigns in Portugal Spain France and America*, (Carlisle G and T Coward LTD, 1914), pp. 64-65.

[118] Ibid., pp. 65-66.

[119] Sherer, Moyle, *Recollections of the Peninsular*, (London, 1823), pp. 161-163.

[120] All of these figures are based on the research by Charles Oman in the appendix of *A History of the Peninsular War, Volume Four*, (Clarendon Press, 1911), p. 634.

[121] Wellesley-Pole to Wellington, 16 June 1811, Raglan Papers, Wellington B #114.

[122] Thompson, Mark S., *Wellington's Engineers: Military Engineering in the Peninsular War 1808-1814*, (Pen and Sword Books, 2015), p. 106.

[123] Grattan, William, *Adventures of the Connaught Rangers From 1808-1814*, (Henry Colburn, 1847), pp. 91-92.

[124] Liddell Hart, B.H (Editor), *The Letters of Private Wheeler 1809-1828*, (The Alden Press, 1998), p. 58.

[125] Ibid., pp. 58-59.

[126] Ibid., p. 59.

[127] Ibid., pp. 60-61.

[128] Grattan, William, *Adventures of the Connaught Rangers From 1808-1814*, (Henry Colburn, 1847), pp. 98-99.

[129] Oman, Charles, *A History of the Peninsular War, Volume Four*, (Clarendon Press, 1911), p. 425.

[130] Ibid., p. 427.

[131] Fraser, Edward, *The Soldiers Whom Wellington Led: Deeds of Daring, Chivalry, and Renown*, (London Methuen, 1913), p. 219.

[132] Grattan, William, *Adventures of the Connaught Rangers From 1808-1814*, (Henry Colburn, 1847), p. 99.

[133] Liddell Hart, B.H (Editor), *The Letters of Private Wheeler 1809-1828*, (The Alden Press, 1998), p. 62.

[134] This poem is quoted by Grattan and attributed to Johnny Newcome.

[135] Donaldson, Joseph, *Recollections of the Eventful Life of a Soldier*, (G.B. Zieber and Co, 1845), p.p. 142-144.

[136] Sherer, Moyle, *Recollections of the Peninsular*, (London, 1823), pp. 172-173.

[137] Sherer, Moyle, *Recollections of the Peninsular*, (London, 1823), pp. 176-177.

[138] One example was John Shipp who was twice promoted from the ranks. I told his story in this popular video on my YouTube channel https://youtu.be/2BNq884wz3E

[139] Oman, Charles, *Wellington's Army (1809-1814)*, (London, Edward Arnold, 1913), p. 198.

[140] Ibid., p. 178.

Printed in Great Britain
by Amazon

32478489R00096